# THE SILVER DRUM
## A JAPANESE IMPERIAL MEMOIR
### – PRINCESS CHICHIBU –

*Princess Chichibu admiring the Prince's beloved
deep-red plum blossoms*

# The Silver Drum
## A Japanese Imperial Memoir
### by
### Setsuko, Princess Chichibu

GLOBAL ORIENTAL

THE SILVER DRUM
A Japanese Imperial Memoir – Princess Chichibu
WITH AN INTRODUCTION BY CARMEN BLACKER

First Published in Japanese:
GIN NO BONBONNIERE
Published by Shufunotomo Co. Ltd.
©1991 by H.I.H. Setsuko, Princess Chichibu

First Published 1996 in English by:
GLOBAL BOOKS LTD
PO Box 219
Folkestone, Kent CT20 3LZ

*Global Oriental is an
imprint of Global Books Ltd*

Translated by Dorothy Britton

©English Translation Dorothy Britton 1996

ISBN 1-86034-004-0

**British Library Cataloguing in Publication Data**
A CIP catalogue entry for this book is available
from the British Library

*Bt
CHICHIBU*

Set in Garamond 12 on 13 point by Bookman, Slough
Printed in England by The Cromwell Press Ltd
Broughton Gifford, Wiltshire

# Contents

# *Preface*

*T*his book records my recollections of eighty-odd years. As they passed by in my mind like the images on a revolving lantern, there were fond, nostalgic memories, joyful ones and amusing ones, and painful and sad ones too. As I tried to recall them, it was as if I were living those 80 years all over again. Some things I could not even bring myself to recount. Every now and again a recollection would break off in the middle as if it had been erased. Some, I would find I had misremembered, and would have to go back and rack my brains again.

At times like that, it was my equerry, Mr Mizoguchi, my private secretary Mr Yamaguchi, and my lady-in-waiting Mrs Shimizu who encouraged me to go on and painstakingly helped me look through old diaries, letters, drafts of poems, and photographs. In particular, I am most grateful to Mr Yamaguchi and Mrs Shimizu for their tireless attendance during the past six months when I have not been well. It is only because of their help that I have been able to follow the sequence of these old recollections. All I had to do was talk while others put it all together, but I often wondered what use there was in recording my memoirs at this late date, and there are some things I have not touched upon at all.

I decided to publish these memoirs because there has been so much written about me that was not true, and I wanted to set the record straight. It was generally believed that the Prince and I were involved in a great romance. The truth of the matter is that if it had not been for the sudden death of Emperor Taisho, the Prince was intending to return to Oxford University, while as for me, an immature and busy high school student in America, romance was the last thing I would have had time for. But wherever I go, that is all that people ask me about.

The facts are as set down in this book, which I hope will give readers some idea of what the Prince was like in the brief time allotted to him on this earth. No one would have been happier than the Prince to see how things have changed and how open and modern the life of the Imperial Family has become. If only he were alive and well now, so that I could know what he thought about it all, and about these memoirs of mine!

My childhood friend Masako Shirasu has been a tower of strength to me in preparing this book. I want to thank her not only for that, but for her long and steadfast friendship.

I am very grateful to Dorothy Britton (Lady Bouchier) for translating these memoirs, and to Dr Carmen Blacker for providing the Introduction. I hope that this little book will bring my old friends nearer, and that it may help to further understanding between our countries.

*Setsuko*
*PRINCESS CHICHIBU*

# *Foreword*

*E*ver since Princess Chichibu's book appeared in Japanese in 1991, her nephew, Prince Tomohito of Mikasa, and I have felt that these unusual memoirs, with their fascinating insights into life in the Imperial Family, should be translated into English so that people abroad could enjoy them too.

Here in Japan, readers have enjoyed Her Highness's memoirs so much that it has not only been issued on cassette for the vision impaired, but has been released in paperback in the popular Kodansha Library series.

His Imperial Highness and I managed to persuade Japan-born author and poet Dorothy Britton (Lady Bouchier) to undertake the task of translation into English, since we felt she had the necessary sensitivity and understanding of things Japanese.

Her Imperial Highness, alas, died on 25 August, and sadly did not live to see the translation of her book in print, but I know that Princess Chichibu's many international friends and admirers will welcome the appearance of this English edition, partly made possible by the generous support of the Japan-British Society.

*Kazuko Aso, DBE*
*SEPTEMBER, 1995*

PUBLISHER'S NOTE

*Japanese names*
The Japanese convention for names is to put the family name first and the given name last; an example would be Matsudaira Katamori as found in Carmen Blacker's scholarly Introduction overleaf. However, to assist the non-specialist reader, this English edition of the Princess' memoir presents names according to the Western convention, that is with the given name first.

*Long vowels*
The romanized version of some Japanese words used in the text carry a line over certain vowels (known as a macron), principally 'o' and 'u'; another way of expressing this elongated sound is by doubling the nominated vowel to 'oo' and 'uu', but this is less commonly used. We have not included the macron in common place names such as Tokyo and Kyushu.

# Introduction

*By Carmen Blacker*

*H*ere is an unusual and remarkable book. Never before has a member of the Japanese Imperial Family written a complete autobiography, and never before have any such memoirs been made available to English readers. But here we have Princess Chichibu, born in 1909, telling of her childhood, her famous grandfather who was a feudal lord, her three years in Washington when her father was Japanese Ambassador to the United States, and eventually her marriage, utterly unexpected, to the Emperor's younger brother in 1928. We are further told of her difficulties of finding herself, untrained in any Court etiquette, suddenly thrown into a world which she had always regarded as inaccessibly remote and 'other', removed 'above the clouds' from ordinary human avocations.

Princess Chichibu was born in Walton-on-Thames while her father, Matsudaira Tsuneo, was an attaché at the Japanese Embassy in London. She returned to Japan after only eight months, however, so that her lifelong regard for England can stem from no conscious memories of an idyllic Edwardian childhood. Perhaps, however, some memory lingered in her subconscious mind, for with her excellent command of English, she has always proved a warm and staunch friend of this country. Indeed, the title of her book, *The Silver Drum*, symbolizes this feeling for Britain. The silver drum in question, a small *bonbonnière* or sweetbox in the shape of a Japanese hand-drum (illustrated on the book jacket), was a present to her from the Empress Dowager, the widow of the Emperor Taishō. Such silver mementos were given by the Japanese Court to mark certain special occasions, much as Fabergé eggs were distributed by the Russian Court at Easter.

But this particular silver box was decorated with motifs which symbolized the friendship of Japan with Britain and America. And all her life, she tells us, it has proved a special treasure, a magic talisman which gave her courage and comfort in moments of difficulty and stress.

Princess Chichibu's grandfather was Matsudaira Katamori, the daimyo or feudal lord of the Aizu domain, whose unwavering support of the tottering Shogunate during the war preceding the Restoration of 1868 marked one of the most dramatic incidents of the whole momentous change. The castle town of Aizu Wakamatsu was besieged by the forces of the new government, and only by dint of the celebrated *Aizu-damashii*, the peculiar tenacious courage on which the samurai class of the Aizu clan prided itself, did the castle hold out for a month against overwhelming odds. The horrors of the campaign and its aftermath were vividly recalled by Dr Willis, the English doctor sent by the new government to render what medical aid he could to the wounded. He heard many tales of the bravery of the Aizu women in the castle during the siege; they cut off their hair, nursed the wounded, and often took a turn with a rifle at the defences of the castle. He saw the daimyo, a dirty and dejected prisoner, leaving for Edo under heavy guard with scarcely a dozen people to witness his departure.

On arrival in Edo he was branded a traitor to the Throne. In the complex web of loyalties of that turbulent time, Princess Chichibu assures us, Katamori was never disloyal to the Emperor, though he opposed tooth and nail the Satsuma and Chōshū clans who engineered the revolutionary change. So devoted was he to the Imperial house, indeed, that he always carried next to his skin, even in a hot bath, the letters written to him by the Emperor Kōmei, sealed in a bamboo tube. The fact that he was branded as a traitor after the fall of the castle was a cause of misery to him for the rest of his life, and he counselled his descendents not to rest until the stain on the honour of the Aizu clan was wiped out.

Accordingly, through her childhood, Princess Chichibu was never allowed to forget the *Aizu-damashii*. She was constantly reminded of the special spirit of the samurai members of her family, and of the wrong done to its honour. She must never waste a grain of rice, for example, but bear in mind the sufferings of the Aizu people in exile.

In 1925 her father was appointed Japanese Ambassador in Washington and she was sent to a much respected Quaker school in the city. She was getting on well with her English and algebra, and during the school holidays she enjoyed waltzing with her father, who liked Caruso and who sang arias from Traviata.

But this happy period was interrupted by the arrival in Washington of Count Kabayama, with a proposal from the Empress Dowager that she should marry Prince Chichibu. The proposal came as a total surprise, not to say a bombshell. She had only met the Prince a couple of times and then their meetings had been marked by no special attention. The first reaction of both her parents and herself was to say no; she was untrained in Court etiquette, unsuitable in every way to take on the responsibilities of consort to an Imperial Prince. The prospect was daunting and terrifying, for to her, as to all Japanese outside it, the Court was an 'other world', remote and discontinuous with all that she was accustomed to.

The Empress Dowager, however, refused to take no for an answer. Back came Count Kabayama on the next boat, with even more pressing proposals. It was only when she remembered the *Aizu-damashii*, and realised that by accepting the proposal she might redeem the honour of the Aizu clan, that she reluctantly gave her consent.

She then found herself thrust, virtually from the schoolroom, into the vortex of a royal network of obligations and behaviour, in which every movement, every minute detail of clothing, every phrase and nuance of language, was almost ritually prescribed. And in which the evening diversion of the Court was not waltzing and singing Verdi, but playing the solemn game of *Nō-karuta*, Nō cards, on which passages from medieval Nō plays were written in difficult calligraphy.

It was not until three months after her wedding that she was able to dine with her parents again *en famille*. She found herself treated as royalty, and addressed with all the correct honorific complexities of the Japanese language. Her old nanny Taka, who had been in the family since she was a child, would not raise her eyes to look at her.

But her marriage with Prince Chichibu proved to be a very happy one, and they quickly became devoted to each other. He had many endearing qualities which she soon came to love and admire. Her life, accordingly, was largely focused on her husband and his work during the 1930s at the Military Academy. He worked so hard that he was often up all night, while she naturally sat up for him in the next room, listening in silence to the calls of the owls.

But historians will learn nothing from her on the vexed question of the part he actually played in the army during the years leading up to the war. Short of making clear that her husband was shocked and angry with the young officers behind the February 26th Incident of 1936, in which a fanatical military faction occupied the centre of Tokyo and murdered three government ministers, we hear little from Princess Chichibu of the ominous signals of growing militarism in Japan.

Her account of the war years is resolutely personal.

We can gather from her narrative, however, that the Prince had little sympathy with the army's fatal policy of war with Britain and America. He received the news of the outbreak of war in silence, and thereafter refused to make any mention of the catastrophe. Now an invalid, he spent much of his time in their mountain villa in Gotemba gazing at Mt Fuji. She, for her part, cultivated a vegetable garden.

Those English readers who might expect more on this subject from the staunch friend of England and America that Princess Chichibu had undoubtedly been all her life, should remember that the book was initially written for Japanese readers, for whom the Imperial

Family has always been outside the turmoil of politics, in that 'world above the clouds' indeed that Princess Chichibu mentions earlier in the book as seeming so remote and inaccessible. That she should make no mention of the broader issues, terrible though they were and terrible though they must have been for herself, is a matter of Court protocol. We know that there are many restrictions on the members of the Imperial Family; among them was the rule that required her when she wrote the book to stick to the purely personal account of their lives during those fateful years.

In her Preface she tells us that there is much more that she could have written, but that she did not choose to do so. We must read between the lines, and remember that special quality of the Japanese language so prized through the centuries: *honomekashi*, or the power of suggesting concentric circles of meaning radiating from the central nucleus of the word. Unfortunately, not even so excellent a translation as Dorothy Britton's can reproduce this quality in English. We might recall, perhaps, that in September 1941 the Emperor was confronted with a group of officers who, in the grip of their powerful and terrifying myth, believed that they knew 'the Emperor's mind' better than he did himself. He chose to quote them a poem composed by his grandfather, the Emperor Meiji:

> Yomo no umi/Mina harakara to/Omou yo ni
> Nado namikaze no/Tachisawaguramu.
>
> *In a world where all within the four seas*
> *are brothers, why should the wind and*
> *waves so furiously rage?*

Prince Chichibu's illness sadly proved incurable, and

he died in 1953. Princess Chichibu's life since his death has been a busy one of charitable works, and travel to promote friendship between Japan and Britain. She has been several times to this country, and visited Magdalen College Oxford where Prince Chichibu studied in the autumn of 1926 before having to return to Japan on account of the illness of his father (Emperor Taishō).

Not long ago I was sorting some old papers and came across what seemed to be an old exercise book compiled in the year 1937. In it were stories and poems and cuttings from the newspapers. There on the first couple of pages were five pictures cut from the *Daily Mail*, of Prince and Princess Chichibu, who had come to England to attend the Coronation of King George VI. I must have been a fan of Princess Chichibu at the age of twelve. It is a special happiness therefore to write hese words of Introduction for Dorothy Britton's tı anslation, *The Silver Drum*. May it bring to English aı.d American readers something of the fascination that Japanese have found in this account of a world from which legends and rumours spring galore, but few such authentic and intriguing recollections.

# Acknowledgements

*T*he translator wishes to thank HIH Prince Tomohito of Mikasa, Mrs Kazuko Aso, Sir Hugh Cortazzi,
Mr Kyōichi Usui, Mr Christopher McDonald, Mr Martyn
Naylor, and others for their assistance and encouragement, especially Mrs Hattori and Mr Yamaguchi who
kindly went through the typescript and made many
helpful suggestions. Thanks are also due to Yoshiko
Tanaka for making available her tape-recording of the
book in Japanese.

# Chronology of Events in the Life of Setsuko, Princess Yasuhito Chichibu

1909    9 September: born in Walton-on-Thames, England.

1910    Returns to Japan in April.

1913    Enters Japanese kindergarten, Peking.

1916    Enters primary school in Japanese Concession, Tientsin.

1918    Returns to Japan.
        Enters Peeresses' School in September.

1925    17 February: leaves for USA, to which father appointed
        Ambassador.
        Enters Friends School in Washington in September.

1928    13 January: name moved to family register of uncle,
        Viscount Morio Matsudaira.
        18 May: Graduates from Friends School.
        1 June: leaves Washington, sailing from San Francisco on
        board the *Shunyo Maru*.
        22 June: arrives in Yokohama.
        14 September: *nōsai-no-gi*, betrothal ceremony, at

Viscount Matsudaira's house.

17 September: Chinese characters for 'Setsuko' changed.

28 September: wedding ceremony and invested with Order of the Sacred Crown, First Class.

17–25 October: visits Ise Grand Shrine and Imperial tombs in Nara and Kyoto.

31 October: visits Tama Imperial Mausoleum.

6–27 November: attends Enthronement ceremonies of Shōwa Emperor Hirohito.

1935 9 August: Prince Chichibu posted to Hirosaki as Commanding Officer, 31st Infantry Regiment.

1936 9 December: Prince Chichibu posted to General Staff, Tokyo.

1937 18 March: Leaves Yokohama aboard *Heian Maru* for Canada, en route to England to attend Coronation of King George VI.

12 May: Receives medal from the King commemorating the Coronation of Their Majesties.

15 October: leaves for Switzerland and the Netherlands, later boarding the *Hikawa Maru* from England for Canada en route back to Japan.

1939 22 May: becomes Honorary President, Japan Anti-Tuberculosis Association.

1940 21 June: Prince Chichibu becomes ill.

1941 16 September: moves to Gotemba.

1952 20 January: moves to Kugenuma.

1953 4 January: death of Prince Chichibu.

24 March: becomes Honorary Vice-President, Japan Red Cross.

13 August: becomes Honorary Patron, Japan-British Society.

6 October: becomes Honorary Patron, Japan-Sweden Society.

1954 15 November: moves to Tokyo.

1962    21 July–7 August: visits Britain and Sweden as Honorary Patron, Japan-British and Japan- Sweden Societies. Also visits Paris.
23 July: created Honorary Dame Grand Cross of the Order of the British Empire.

1967    27 January–7 February: as Honorary Patron, Japan-British Society, visits Britain to attend 75th anniversary celebration in London of the Japan Society.

1969    8 April: invested by the King of Sweden with the Grand Cordon of the Order of the Seraphim.
1 October: becomes Honorary President of the Association for Traffic Accident Orphans.

1970    8–9 May: visits Korea together with Prince and Princess Takamatsu to attend the funeral of Princess Li of the former Royal House.

1974    7–19 June: visits Britain at the invitation of the British Government.

1978    9 October: invested by Princess Margaret at the British Embassy on behalf of Her Majesty the Queen as Honorary Dame Grand Cross of the Order of St Michael and St George.

1979    4–18 June: visits Britain at the invitation of the British Government, returning via the USA.

1980    19 February: is made an Honorary Fellow of the Royal Horticultural Society.

1981    17–18 October: visits Britain at the invitation of the British Government to attend the opening of the Great Japan Exhibition in London, and also visits Switzerland.

1985    4–11 March: visits Nepal at the invitation of the Nepalese Government, returning via Thailand.

# Glossary of Japanese Words

| | |
|---|---|
| *anpan* | Soft bread rolls with sweetened *azuki*-paste centre. From *an*, bean-jam, and *pan*, bread, from Portuguese *pão*. |
| *azuki* | Tiny reddish-brown beans. Adzuki or aduki in English. |
| *banzai* | Hurrah! May you (he, she, etc) live long! |
| *daijōsai* | The ancient mystical rite of all-night communion with the spirits of his ancestors observed by a new emperor on his enthronement. |
| *furisode* | Brightly coloured formal kimono with long sleeves worn by young unmarried women. |
| *furoshiki* | Square cloth used for wrapping things. |
| *go* | Intricate game for two played with black and white stones on a board, competing for territory. Also called *igo*. |
| *hakama* | Ankle-length pleated divided-skirt worn over kimono by men or women. |
| *hamon* | Temper-pattern on the blade of a Japanese sword. |

| | |
|---|---|
| *haori-hakama* | Men's full-dress formal wear of, say, grey silk *hakama* and black silk kimono-type jacket (*haori*) bearing family crests. |
| *hitoe* | Unlined. |
| *honomekashi* | Hint; suggestion; allusion. |
| *hori-gotatsu* | *Kotatsu* (see below) having a sunken pit under it which enables sitter to put his or her feet down upon the warming device, while sitting on the tatami floor. |
| *itsutsuginu* | Five silken robes. Nowadays just one simulating five. |
| *jūnihitoe* | Ancient costume originally comprising twelve robes. |
| *karaginu* | Brocade jacket worn over the 'Twelve-layered robe'. |
| *Kashiko-dokoro* | Sanctuary in the Imperial Palace grounds. |
| *Kempeitai* | The former dreaded military police whose reputation for cruelty and injustice is still a byword. |
| *kogin* | Traditiuonal handcrafted fabric made in Hirosaki. Dark blue homespun linen with patterns worked into weave in white yarn. |
| *kosode* | Short-sleeved kimono. |
| *kotatsu* | Quilt-covered, table-topped framework holding a heat source for warming the knees as one sits on the tatami floor. |
| *kunen-shu* | A ceremonial thick black *sake* made by boiling black soybeans, ordinary *sake* and *mirin* (sweet *sake*). |
| *mikagura* | Sacred Shintō music and dances performed at shrines. |
| *mirin* | A sweet *sake*, mostly used in cooking. |
| *monpe* | Jacket and baggy pants of splash-patterned indigo cloth worn over kimono for farm work. |
| *naga-bakama* | Full and very long *hakama* (see above) worn with ancient 'Twelve-layered robe'. |
| *nōsai-no-gi* | Ceremonial exchange of betrothal gifts. |

| | |
|---|---|
| *o-shiruko* | Thick sweet warm drink made with *azuki*-bean paste and served with rice cakes (*mochi*). |
| *obi* | Sash. |
| *rakugo* | Traditional art of comic story-telling. |
| *sake* | Alcoholic beverage brewed from fermented rice. |
| *sembei* | Rice crackers. |
| *setsu* | Season. |
| *shichiriki* | Ancient flute. |
| *shō* | Ancient mouth-organ. |
| *shōgi* | Japanese chess. |
| *sukiyaki* | Paper-thin slices of beef cooked with vegetables, *tōfu*, etc., and soy sauce and sweet *sake*, in a chafing-dish at table. |
| *sushi* | Vinegared rice with fish, vegetables, seaweed etc. |
| *susuki* | *Miscanthus sinensis*, a kind of pampas grass. |
| *tabi* | Foot mittens. |
| *tanka* | Literally 'short poem', and also called *waka*, 'Japanese poem', 31 syllables in five lines of 5,7,5,7,7 – in effect a triplet and a couplet. The triplet led to the three-line haiku. |
| *tokonoma* | Ornamental recess in sitting/dining-room designed for display of hanging scroll, single art object and flower arrangement. |
| *tsuzumi* | Hourglass-shaped hand-drum. |
| *uchiginu, uchiki* | Two of the many robes of the *jūnihitoe* court costume. |
| *uwagi* | Outer garment; coat. |
| *waka* | See *tanka* (above). |
| *washi* | Japanese handmade paper. |

# CHAPTER ONE

# Birth and Background

## AN AUSPICIOUS BIRTHDAY

*I* was born in England, in the town of Walton-on-Thames, not far from London, at the ninth hour of the ninth day of the ninth month of the year nineteen hundred and nine – five nines, and very auspicious!

Japan still celebrates some of the ancient Chinese seasonal festivals based on the lunar calendar, and the Chrysanthemum Festival on the ninth day of the ninth month is considered particularly favourable. Its Chinese name signifies 'much yang' – yang symbolizing the sun, brightness, and the positive principle. At the court in ancient Japan, they used to hold a banquet on the day of the Chrysanthemum Festival and wine was served to the guests in which chrysanthemums had been steeped, for the chrysanthemum is said to promote long life.

So I was named Setsu, which means 'Season' and is the first character in 'seasonal festival'. *Setsu* also means moderation and restraint, a nice word.

My father was Third Secretary at the Japanese Embassy in London when I was born, and my brother Ichiro had been born there, too, the previous year. My mother Nobuko, daughter of Marquis Nabeshima, had travelled all the way to London from Japan to marry my father, whom she had never met. There was no opportunity since she was in Tokyo and he in London, so only photographs were exchanged. The marriage had been arranged between their two families, as in feudal times.

My brothers and I used to tease Mother and call her a 'picture bride' but our parents had both had a modern education and were not the sort of people to let themselves be coerced into marrying someone they did not fancy, so they must have liked what they saw in those photographs and what they knew about one another.

My earliest memories go back to when I was four, in Peking, the year after my sister was born there, and the arrival of Mutsu Takahashi – the beloved nanny we called 'Taka' and came to look upon as a member of the family. She had lost her husband in the Russo-Japanese War and was teaching at a primary school when she was recommended to my parents as just the person to look after us three children. Moreover, she came from a family who belonged to the former Aizu clan.

THE AIZU CLAN

My father, Tsuneo Matsudaira, was the fourth son of Katamori Matsudaira, Lord of the former feudal domain of Aizu, who had been unjustly accused of being a traitor to the Emperor.

'Might is right', as the saying goes, and my grandfather was on the wrong side: a victim of circumstance in the struggle for the overthrow of the Tokugawa shogunate – the military government of Japan that lasted from 1600 to 1868.

Far from being a traitor, my grandfather's loyalty to the Emperor was beyond question, and the Emperor held him in high regard. My grandfather, in the service of the Shogun, was in charge of the defence of Kyoto, where the Emperor resided, and we have a long, confidential letter that he once received from Emperor Kōmei himself.

'Thou hast exerted thyself mightily on our behalf and we are well pleased', begins part of the missive, and goes on:

'Thy loyalty is such that even our most secret and confidential thoughts may be safely entrusted to thee, and moreover we have asked thee to undertake this matter because we are confident that whatsoever we desire can be brought to pass by thy skilful manoeuvering in the art of bringing about the agreement of many.'

In order to maintain secrecy, the Emperor composed his letter in the form of an Imperial poem in classical Chinese and sent it to my grandfather by special messenger in a ceremonial lacquer scroll box to make it appear as if he were merely bestowing an Imperial gift of a poem.

To Katamori, who had been held in such a position of deep trust, the sudden death in 1866 of the young, 36-year-old Emperor Kōmei, must have been a bitter blow in that time of great upheaval, with its plots and counter-plots and divergent opinions regarding the future of Japan.

The overthrow of the Shogunate and the restoration of power to the Emperor had been planned by men of the far-flung domains of Satsuma and Chōshū. The

Lord of Satsuma was well aware of my grandfather Katamori's unswerving loyalty to the Emperor, but he also knew that the Lord of Aizu owed allegiance to the Shogun, in his capacity as the defender of Imperial Kyoto.

There was therefore no way for my grandfather to escape being considered an enemy. In the civil war that followed, the Aizu clan came under heavy attack by the Imperial Restoration forces, made up largely of Satsuma and Chōshū men, under the command of Taruhito, Prince Arisugawa.

The heroism of the Byakkotai – the White Tiger Brigade – is legendary. Of that band of several hundred young sons of Aizu samurai, twenty survivors saw in the distance their castle in flames, and committed suicide.

Women and children fought side by side with the men in the desperate, month-long defence of Wakamatsu Castle until finally the white flag of surrender was carried out through the North Gate. From that time on, there was nothing but hardship and humiliation for the Aizu Clan. After surrendering Wakamatsu Castle, my grandfather, whose initial death penalty was commuted to life imprisonment, was taken to Tokyo to be held prisoner in the manor of the Lord of Tottori, and all of his lands were confiscated.

The new Imperial government, however, lifted the sentence in less than a year. Then, as well as recognizing Katamori's eldest son Kataharu as the head of the house of Matsudaira, they bestowed on him the fief of Tonami on the Shimokita peninsula in the province of Mutsu (present-day Aomori Prefecture).

It was a poor fief in undeveloped country that could only produce 150,000 bushels of rice a year at best – a shabby exchange for a major domain that produced

400,000 bushels! It was tantamount to exile. Some of the clansmen, including my uncle Kataharu, travelled there by boat from Niigata, while others made their way north by road. The members of the aizu clan were obliged to lead a harsh life there for five years before they were allowed, in 1873, to return to Aizu and earn a proper living.

Although my grandfather Katamori was pardoned in 1870, he stubbornly refused to accept public office again. In November, 1874, Emperor Meiji personally requested that he be made a courtier of the fifth rank, from which he was promoted subsequently to the senior grade of the Third Court rank, but while he had the greatest respect for Emperor Meiji, he continued to harbour a deep resentment against those whose might had made them right.

My father, Tsuneo, was born in a suburb of Tokyo in April, 1875. By that time, although the tragedy suffered by the Aizu clan had left a deep hurt that remained in the people's hearts, most of the former clansmen went along with the times and were beginning to make a new life for themselves.

Tsuneo was about seven when his parents took him back to live in their ancestral home, the old castle town of Wakamatsu in their former Aizu domain. His younger brother Morio went too. His three elder brothers, Kataharu, Takeo and Hideo, who had experienced all the hardships of Tonami, were farmed out to various members of the former clan who lived in Tokyo, in order to pursue their education.

The journey to Wakamatsu from Tokyo was made in a procession of twenty rickshaws. Their destination was the Herb Garden. It was a sort of country villa belonging to His Lordship, with a magnificent kitchen garden where many herbs were grown. The property had been sadly neglected, but repairs were made and the family took up residence there.

The local primary school was about half a mile from the Herb Garden, and my father used to tell of the ordeal it had been in winter, walking there over the frozen snow on the footpaths between the rice paddies, wearing only wooden clogs on their bare feet. Sometimes there were blizzards, too. The school was an old-fashioned institution of the temple school variety, with tatami-matted floors, and father often made us laugh about how the first thing the teacher taught them was the fact that '*T'soon rises in t' East, and gaws dahn in t' West*', spoken in rich local dialect.

My father spent about three years in Aizu, after which he was to rejoin his parents in Tokyo, but during his primary school days there, the scars of the Battle of Aizu were still far from healed, and mixing freely as he did with the local children, he heard from them of the suffering their families had endured. It was learning about it at first hand, I think, that gave him his spiritual strength and the deep love for his ancestral province, which in due course he passed on to us children.

The day they left Aizu behind to move to Tokyo, my grandfather's former retainers followed the cavalcade of tandem rickshaws in a long line for mile after mile, and even when night fell, their lanterns formed a continuous stream of light, for they could not bear to tear themselves away. To the former clansmen, my grandfather was still their lord and master. My grandfather finally had to dismount from his carriage, and say: 'You mustn't come with us any further. You must go home now. Let us part here.' It was not until then that they finally stopped following.

Although my father was still a child, the pathos of that night's sad parting of lord and vassals made a deep impression upon him. Sitting in the carriage beside his younger brother Morio, and looking back through tear-filled eyes at the light of those lanterns, he determined in his heart that for the sake of these people of Aizu he must make something of himself so that they could be proud of him.

My father did not tell me this himself, but told my cousins, adding: 'You are Matsudairas too. You must never forget the people of Aizu.' My cousins had just lost their father, and their uncle was trying to encourage them.

After returning to our mansion in Tokyo's Koishika-wa, my father was sent to the nearby Kuroda Primary School for a year in order to rid him of his Aizu accent. It would never do for him to say '*T'soon gaws dahn in t'West*' at the Gakushūin, the Peers' School, where the sons of the Imperial Family and the nobility went.

From Gakushūin, he would go on to the First High School, and then to the Tokyo Imperial University, graduating in 1902 and entering the Foreign Ministry. In the meantime, in 1892, my grandfather Katamori's stormy life came to an end. Only then, I believe, did the feudal era truly end for the people of Aizu.

After spending two years in Peking, my father was appointed Consul-General in Tientsin, where each nation had its own Concession under the Treaty of Extraterritoriality. We lived in the British Concession, and my brother and I had to be taken by rickshaw each day through the French Concession to the Japanese primary school, which was at the far end of the Japanese Concession. It took us awhile to get to school, and when we dawdled over our breakfast, Taka would hurry us up with her favourite expression: 'Come on, or the castle will fall!'

While in Tientsin I learned a valuable lesson.

Overawed by the rough-and-tumble crowd of boys and girls, I was too timid to push my way past them during break to take a drink of water in the overpowering heat of summer. No matter how unbearably thirsty I was, I just stubbornly endured it, not even daring to confide in my brother. One day, I collapsed with heatstroke and was unconscious for nearly three weeks. When I finally recovered, our father sent for us both and gave us a stern talking to, pointing out that while the brave endurance of suffering was an admirable Aizu trait, being able to speak out and look after one's own and other's welfare was also an important part of the Aizu spirit. I have never forgotten his words, and they have stood me in good stead in my life at Court.

CHAPTER TWO

# *Growing Up*

THE PEERESSES' SCHOOL

*W*e returned to Japan in 1918. My father had been appointed Councillor to the Embassy in Washington, and we were all to have gone back together, prior to setting out for the United States. However, plans changed. The Revolution having started in Russia, Siberia was in an unsettled state, and Japan, as one of the Allies in World War I had declared its intention of sending troops there, and my father was asked by the Foreign Ministry to go alone to Vladivostok as Political Affairs Adviser to the expeditionary army. So the rest of us went back to Japan without him.

After spending some time at another school improving my Japanese manners, I finally passed the entrance examination to the Primary Department of the Peeresses' School, where mother wanted me to go. In the meantime, my father had returned from Vladivostok and was put in charge of the European and American Bureau at the Foreign Ministry.

I used to walk to school most days from our home across what were then the wide open Aoyama fields. I remember how lovely they were, especially in spring with wild flowers and butterflies. As summer turned to autumn, we would chase grasshoppers; and oh,how beautiful the fields were in autumn, with silver *susuki*, a kind of pampas-grass. In winter, cold winds blew across the vast expanse, and when the paths were obliterated by snow, one could easily slip and fall unless one carefully traced previous footprints. If I was late, I took the tram.

The first time I rode on the tram to school, and the next two or three times, my nanny, Taka, went with me, but after that I rode on the tram alone, and with the season-ticket she had bought me in my purse, I felt quite grown-up and very happy. I had an aluminium lunch box in my bag as well as my school books. My lunch contained nothing fancy, and when I came home from school Taka would look inside the box to make sure I had eaten it all, for I was not allowed to leave anything. She severely scolded me once for leaving one or two grains of rice.

'Do you realize that the Aizu clan members in virtual exile on the Tonami Peninsula, and their wives and children, had to live on weeds and grass seeds and the tofu lees and leftover rice, usually fed to horses and oxen, which they were given by the local farmers? Even His Lordship had to make do with this animal fodder, and it was filled with maggots, too. So you keep that in your mind,and don't you leave any rice grains!'

Taka made me so deeply aware in my childish mind of how the Aizu clan felt, that after that, I never left anything – and not only in my school lunch.

Taka always referred to my father as His Lordship,

although it was his brother Kataharu – who had shared the rigours of Tonami with the clan – who first inherited the clan leadership, and when Kataharu died in 1910, my father abdicated the title, that should have come to him, in favour of his younger brother Morio, who was now Lord Matsudaira.

When I was in my early teens, there was a game that was very popular called 'Cormorant's eyes, hawk's eyes'. My elder brother learned it somewhere, and used to be the leader and organized us in playing it, and not only did we children take part, but mother and Taka and some of the maids, too, taking it quite seriously.

My brother, as leader, would place a tray on a table in the large room upstairs. On the tray there would be a set number of objects – say ten things, perhaps, such as a cup and a teapot and things like that. A large cloth would be placed over the tray so the contents could not be seen.

'Ready!' the leader would announce in a solemn voice, and up we would go, one at a time, to be told: 'Now then, carefully observe the objects on the tray and then make a list of them.' Whereupon, he would whip the cloth away, leaving it off for only the space of one breath before covering the tray again. One only had time to glance at the objects before trying to list them. The person who remembered the most objects correctly was the winner. But although one had seen them only the moment before, it was strange how little one could remember. He would start with only three objects, and even then some of us could not remember them all. No matter how hard one tried, staring at the objects with the concentration of cormorants and hawks, it would be almost impossible to recollect what there had been on the tray.

After a while we got the hang of it, and managed to

list more of the things. Memory, concentration, and observation improved with practise. As games go, I feel it ranks high. And besides, it was fun. It is not difficult, but you cannot succeed without concentration. I think children ought to play it today, and it would be good for the elderly, too.

THE GREAT KANTO EARTHQUAKE

The summer of 1923, after the usual fortnight with my best friend Masako at the Kabayama's villa in Gotemba, I spent a while as usual in Oiso at the Nabeshima villa with my grandmother, Marchioness Nabeshima, my cousins, my elder brother and younger sister, and Taka, having fun at the seaside. Then, when the summer holidays were almost over and I still had some unfinished homework to do, I returned to Tokyo. The next day, 1 September, was the day of the Great Earthquake. there is no telling what would have happened to me if I had not gone back to Tokyo, since the Oiso house was completely destroyed.

My sister Masako wanted to stay in Oiso until the very end of the holidays and stayed behind with Taka and we had no news of them for almost a fortnight. We were beside ourselves with worry. Communications were not what they are now, and since telephone lines were down, there was nothing one could do.

Fortunately, our relatives turned out to have survived, but many people lost their lives, including classmates of mine, and countless people were injured and lost their homes. The news that gradually filtered through, was heartbreaking. We heard that the elder sister of Princess Kan'in had been killed at her villa in Odawara. We were terribly worried about Masako Kabayama in Gotemba, and I shall never forget the relief we felt when we heard that she was safe.

On the day of the earthquake I was in my room doing my homework. I heard a roar that seemed to be coming up from the bowels of the earth and suddenly the room started shaking up and down and sideways. I was thrown out of my chair and rolled about, and remembering being taught to get under a table in an earthquake, I grabbed the legs of my desk and rolled under it. As I did so, the house started to collapse. I wasn't scared so much as in a state of shock, so much so that I could not even cry out for help, but simply waited until somebody came and rescued me and took me outside. I was in such a daze I could scarcely think.

After the second big aftershock, we all took refuge in Prince Nashimoto's palace nearby. My mother's sister Itsuko was married to the Prince. The main building had not even lost a single tile, while the annex had only lost a few. Scary aftershocks continued intermittently, so we spent an uneasy night in a tent set up in a bamboo grove on the grounds. Bamboo groves have always been considered the safest place. fires could be seen blazing in various directions, which seemed to be spreading. Prince Li – heir to the throne of Korea – and Masako, his Japanese princess, joined us in our refuge. Aoyama Avenue was said to be a sea of flames, and a great many people whose homes were burned fled to the palace grounds.

Thinking back on it now, I realize it must have been because I was a child, but in spite of all the turmoil, I remember curling up in the tent, sharing a quilt with my cousin Princess Noriko – who was only two years older than I – and falling fast asleep as if I had not a care in the world.

We lived in a sewage pipe for a while afterwards, which was great fun as far as I was concerned. My father was chief of the European and American Affairs Bureau of the Foreign Ministry, and since people from the Ministry and others would doubtless be coming to see him, he felt he could not stay away from the house too long, so, escorted by a secretary from the Prince's household, we went home. Fortunately the house had escaped being burned, but it was uninhabitable. So we copied our neighbours and took shelter in the sewage pipes that workmen had left in the road – living like hermit crabs or snails!

Sewage construction happened to be underway in Tokyo just at that time, and all along the road where we lived, the pipes had been set out ready to be laid down. The pipes were large, and so there was no danger of them sliding into cracks in the ground that might open with further earth tremors, nor would they break apart, since they were made of iron.

Pipes were lying in front of every house, so there were plenty to take shelter in. Lengths of cloth were hung at each end for privacy. Ours had a sheet of paper with 'Matsudaira' written on it hanging at one end, but a man from the Foreign Ministry failed to notice the sign and went to the Nashimoto estate where he expected we would be. When Princess Itsuko Nashimoto heard an equerry say, 'I think they are still in the sewer pipe', she was both alarmed and intrigued, wondering how on earth we would lie down to sleep. That night, escorted by two guards, it seems the princess, together with Princess Noriko, stole out incognito to see how we were faring. After satisfying themselves that all was well, they returned without saying a word to us. when we heard about it afterwards, we agreed that it was just like Princess Itsuko to do a thing like that.

By the time Masako and Taka had returned to Tokyo

our house was more or less fit to live in; Taka suggested that I should tour the earthquake damage. What I saw made a deep impression on me which I shall never forget. It was a real eye-opener.

'This kind of disaster must never happen again,' she said, 'but since it has happened, I think it is useful to see with one's own eyes and clearly understand the extent of the calamity and the misery. I will take her myself and accept full responsibility'.

Mother approved of Taka's proposal and agreed, but said my father should under no circumstances be told. Although it was some time since the earthquake, he would be bound to oppose it, saying that the cruel sight of the burnt ruins of what was once a city would be too much for the sensibilities of a fourteen-year-old girl. Besides, he was sure to argue that law and order was not yet properly established.

On the day of the tour, they dressed me in a plain coarse cotton kimono and *tabi* (Japanese foot-mittens) and clogs to protect my feet. The idea was not to wear Western-style clothes or anything conspicuous, but to resemble the ordinary children of the burnt-out area.

Taka and I – just the two of us – slipped quietly out of the house in Aoyama. We went via Kudan and Nihonbashi, finally walking as far as Ueno. It was hard walking in unfamiliar clothing, and not being used to walking in clogs, I got very tired. It was hard going, and I marvel even now at my perseverance.

Most of the bodies had been cleared away, but there were some left, and I wanted to close my eyes, but instead Taka insisted that I fold my hands and join her in prayer for them. There was no sign of anyone in Nihonbashi, except for a few corpses still floating in the river. Harrowing scenes like that engraved themselves on my young mind. Although I was already familiar with tragic stories of the fall of Wakamatsu Castle, it had all faded into the past and seemed no more than a bad dream, whereas this was naked truth – something I was seeing with my own eyes.

My mother worried terribly, wondering if she had done the right thing to let me go; wondering if the impressions I would receive might not be too much for me; terrified for fear something awful might have happened to us. It was not until we arrived home safely sometime after three o'clock that she was able to stop worrying.

That night, the horrors I had seen did in fact keep me awake until the early hours.

THE AIZU SPIRIT

I think it must have been about a year after the Great Earthquake. I had finished studying, and I do not remember what I wanted there, but on drawing aside the sliding door to the sitting-room, I saw my father, who had just come home, seated on the matted floor holding a drawn sword under the electric light and looking intently at the blade's *hamon*, or temper-pattern.

'Oh, dear! you do look fierce with that sword!,' I blurted out without thinking.

He chided me immediately. 'What a thing for a girl of samurai stock to say! The sight of a sword shouldn't frighten anyone with Aizu blood in their veins!'

I knelt down beside him, abashed.

'When Aizu Castle fell, girls younger than you bravely stabbed themselves to death alongside their mothers and their younger brothers and sisters out of loyalty to your grandfather. You must never forget how shamefully treated your grandfather was, and how much the Aizu people suffered.'

I remember clearly to this day that revelation of a side of my father I had never seen before. I had encountered the Aizu spirit that dwelt in the recesses of my father's soul.

The reason my father had abdicated the headship of the family in favour of his younger brother Morio, declining a title for himself, was because he wanted to start from scratch as an ordinary citizen and member of society. He was determined to make a life for himself by his own efforts. He felt that out of respect for the people who had given such loyalty and devotion to his father, Katamori, he had no right to choose the easy path.

And yet, although he told us never to forget the Aizu spirit of our clansmen and their families, he never exhorted his children to strive to get ahead in the world because of it. I think he always just wanted us to be ordinary, good and upright human beings.

But his reprimand that night, as he gazed so steadfastly at the beautiful, gleaming swordblade he held, made me deeply aware of the Aizu blood that coursed through my veins too.

My father had just been appointed to the highly important post of Under-Secretary for Foreign Affairs. It was a time when relations with the United States were becoming difficult. Looking back now, I wonder if he was not gazing at that swordblade hoping its gleam would help to clear his overcast spirit and calm his mind.

Taka never lost an opportunity to talk to my brother and me about the Aizu spirit.

'The reason so many eminent people come from Aizu,' she would say, 'is because of the defiance of the Aizu men who were treated so badly on the Shimokita

Peninsula by the Meiji government. They were proud, and their Aizu spirit burned within them. They said, "We'll show them, we will!" It was the same with the women. Look at Miss Sutematsu Yamakawa!'

Sutematsu Yamakawa – later the wife of Field Marshall Iwao Oyama – went to Vassar College in America in 1871, when she was 12. She was one of the first Japanese women to study abroad in a group that included Umeko Tsuda, founder of Tsuda College. Miss Yamakawa returned to Japan in 1882, and even after she became Mrs Oyama she was active in social work, in the Red Cross Volunteer Nursing Association and the Womens Patriotic Association. Before Taka came to look after us children, she had taught school and been a nurse, and she had worked in the Womens Patriotic Association, so to her, Sutematsu Yamakawa Oyama was an object of considerable veneration.

My grandfather Katamori, the former Lord of Aizu, spent the last years of his life as High Priest of the Tōshōgū Shrine in Nikko. When he died in Nikko in 1893, he was found to have on his person the two Imperial letters he had once personally received from Emperor Kōmei. According to my brother, the Meiji Government – which consisted almost entirely of Satsuma and Chōshū men – was greatly embarrassed to have Katamori Matsudaira of Aizu in possession of such documents, and while he was alive, repeated attempts were made to retrieve them. But my grandfather was determined that these proofs of Aizu's loyalty to the Imperial House must be preserved at all cost. The Government even offered him a large sum of money for the letters, but Katamori remained adamant. Not knowing when he might be killed by an assassin and the letters stolen, he placed them in a bamboo tube which he wore next to his skin even while bathing.

Ever since then, the Imperial letters have been a treasured heirloom of the Matsudaira family – nay, of the whole Aizu clan – and I believe they will always be a symbol of the Aizu spirit no matter how things may change over the centuries.

## SUMMER IN NIKKO

In my days at the Peeresses' School I was neither an honour student nor a particularly exemplary one. I was certainly not a 'swot'; I simply did whatever I had to do to the best of my ability, and I was industrious. The precepts my father gave me were, 'Do what is right and proper' and 'Do the best you can', and I did my best to follow them.

Foreign language study began in the first year of middle school, and one had to choose between English and French. I talked it over with my mother, who said: 'From your father on, we've all gone in for English in the family and no-one has taken up French, so I think it might be a good idea for one of us to learn to speak French.'

My choosing French was as simple as that. Ten of us, including Princess Kan'in, began learning the language from a Japanese teacher. However, I hardly got anywhere before I had to stop, for in less than a year, my father was appointed ambassador to the United States.

How I regretted not having chosen English instead of French! But after marrying into the Imperial Family, I was grateful for even my small knowledge of French, since it was the lingua franca of royalty. That was obviously why the princesses studied it, although at the time, little did I know that I would be needing the knowledge for the same reason.

What concerned me most as I entered First Year Middle was that my best friend, Masako Kabayama, was leaving, on her own volition, to study in America. How enterprising of her, I thought. While I of course admired Sutematsu Yamakawa, the Aizu woman Taka was so proud of who had gone abroad to study at the age of twelve, here was a contemporary of mine doing the same thing! Furthermore, while Sutematsu was part of a group, Masako would travel across the sea alone to go to a residential college in New Jersey. Taka was impressed. 'What a wonderful young lady!' she said. Taka loved Masako's open-hearted, lively temperament, and for her part, Masako says, 'Taka always treated me quite impartially, and was so good to me, in spite of my being a child of the enemy!'

Masako's family came from Kagoshima – the former Satsuma fief – and her grandfather had taken part in the attack on Aizu. The Aizu spirit burned with a vengeance in Taka's heart, and she was devoted to the memory of my grandfather, whom she called the Great Lord of Aizu. But while Masako was, indeed, a 'child of the enemy', that fierce Taka made an exception in her case and regarded my friend in a special light. Perhaps it was because they were both forthright people who hated flattery and obsequiousness.

I had always looked forward to our annual fortnight in Gotemba with Masako and her family, but that year we visited the Nabeshima villa in Nikko instead. My grandparents like to walk, so we used to hike to see the waterfalls and Lake Chūsenji and Yumoto. We never used any form of transport. This time I saw the famous Kegon Falls for the first time.

One day, mother took me and my younger sister Masako to pay our respects at the Imperial villa near Rinnoji Temple. We were graciously received in audience by Empress Teimei. The Imperial villa was not far from the Nabeshima villa, so there was no problem about walking there in our best kimonos. Mine bore our family crest and had medium-length sleeves. Mother had had it made from a bolt of purple silk gauze she had received from the Empress. My sister wore Western dress, as I remember.

I used to have a photograph of the two of us with young Prince Sumi – as Prince Mikasa was then called – in the middle, but unfortunately it was destroyed in the World War II firebombing. We had been sitting politely, minding our Ps and Qs, when the prince had come over to us and said: 'Let's go out in the garden, and I'll take your picture.'

We went out, and stood in front of a lovely clear stream. Holding his camera, His Highness asked us to move a little this way or that way, and then just as we were expe :ting him to take our photograph, he handed the camera to a flunky, saying, 'press this', and ran over and got in between my sister and me. So instead of the prince taking our picture, it was he who had his picture taken with us girls! The Emperor watched it all with evident enjoyment from an upstairs window.

I did not meet Prince Chichibu that day, as he was not in Nikko, being away, in the army.

It was not unusual for young people to be invited to the Imperial villa or the palace by Her Majesty. When a diplomat was posted abroad as ambassador or minister or some other capacity and their children were old enough, or when the daughter of someone in her service entered high-school, or graduated, Her Majesty would often command her parents to 'bring them too'.

When my mother returned from London, Her Majesty used to summon her often to the palace to help in connection with foreign etiquette and other foreign matters, and when mother returned from Tientsin she was formally appointed to serve at Court. Consequently, as Masako and I grew older, it became a common occurrence for mother to be commanded to bring us too.

## THE DAY I FIRST MET PRINCE CHICHIBU

I never heard any talk at home about who was being considered as a possible bride for Prince Chichibu, but I remember the girls in my class gossiping and speculating about one or two of the young noblewomen who seemed in our inexperienced eyes to have the requisite brains, personality and beauty. It was rumoured that the Empress had visited the Peeresses' School and had spotted a girl she fancied as a bride for her second son.

Empress Teimei – like Empress Shōken, the wife of Emperor Meiji – always attended graduation ceremonies, and often visited classroom sessions, where she would be given a list of the pupils. Girls were not told ahead of time that she was coming and no previous arrangements were made as to what questions would be asked of whom and who would answer. she observed ordinary classes conducted as they normally were. Nor were classes interrupted when Her Majesty entered the room nor obeisances made. We were usually quite unaware of Her Majesty's presence. It did not happen very often. Only about once or twice a year.

It never occurred to us that the purpose of her visits was to find brides. We were simply grateful that she took an interest in us, and it put us on our mettle and made us mind our manners and try harder to be serious in our work so as not to fail.

The first time I was presented to His Imperial highness Prince Yasuhito Chichibu was in February, 1925, when Her Majesty the Empress invited us to the palace shortly before my father was to proceed with his family to the United States as Envoy Extraordinary and Ambassador Plenipotentiary.

My mother, a I remember, wore afternoon dress, and Masako and I went in *furisode* – young girls' gaily coloured party kimonos with flowing sleeves. The Empress received us warmly, and complimented us on our apparel. 'Nobuko,' she said, 'since you are the Ambassador's wife, you will, I suppose, have to dress and wear your hair in Western style, but I hope Setsuko will not have her hair waved, or anything like that.'

That morning, ordered by my mother, Taka had shaved the down from my face and from the nape of my neck for the very first time. 'It tickles,' I had complained, hunching up my shoulders, and Taka had told me crossly not to make such a fuss. I thought of it as the Empress spoke, and felt very grown up.

My first impression of His Highness the Prince was the sparkle of his glasses and his fine, tall figure.

My mother was bidden to the palace once more by Her Majesty, and took me with her, but on that occasion Prince Chichibu was away on a trip and I did not see him.

But as it happened, I met him again quite by chance in an unexpected place, at an unexpected time.

We were ready to sail for America and our baggage had all gone off, but a bad storm was predicted and our ship's departure was postponed. Mother suggested that father take us two girls to Nagaoka on the Izu Peninsula to fill in the time before the ship's departure, so off we went. It was the first time we had gone anywhere just by ourselves, with no servants, and we three boarded the train in the highest of spirits. The train was packed, and we had great difficulty finding seats. When we finally did, who should be in the same carriage but Prince Chichibu!

His Highness was in the uniform of an infantry cadet and was accompanied by an aide. My father went up to pay his respects, with my sister and me following behind. The Prince acknowledged our rather stiff bows with a slight nod and asked where we were going. I think my father explained about our ship having been delayed, but I do not remember anything else about the meeting at all. I was so happy to be going on a journey with father that it must have absorbed all my attention. Before getting off the train at Nagaoka, we followed father again in taking leave of the Prince.

What we enjoyed most about those two or three days in Nagaoka was being with father from morning to night. In the peaceful countryside, standing on a bridge over a stream near the hills, using us for an audience, father practised the speech in English that he would give on arriving in Washington.

He rehearsed the speech aloud every day, and each time, when he had finished, he asked us, a little shyly, what we thought of it.

'Well', we would say, trying to sound wise, 'it still sounds a bit flat. Shouldn't you put a little more expression into it?' And taking us quite seriously, he would reply, 'I see,' and, clearing his throat, he would start again from the beginning. I can still hear him now, in my mind, and I cherish the memory.

# CHAPTER THREE

# *America*

## THE REUNION

*T*he danger of the storm being over, we sailed from Yokohama on board the Tōyō Steamship Company's Taiyō Maru on 17 February 1925. I was only fifteen, and at that tender age I found it heartbreakingly sad to leave my elder brother behind all by himself and sail away from my homeland for a far country. It was my first experience of parting and separation.

Taka's daughter Chie was travelling with us. When Taka came to us as our Nanny, her son Ryō was eleven and her daughter Chie was nine. Raised by our grandparents, when they were old enough, they came to Tokyo too, and entered Aoyama Gakuin school. Chie was already twenty-one, and having been at Aoyama Gakuin she could speak English, and was an ideal assistant to Taka.

The Taiyō Maru arrived in San Francisco on time, and from there we spent eight days on a train and reached Washington on 11 March. We were met at the station by Embassy staff and driven to the Japanese Embassy residence.

As we began our life in Washington, the thing that worried me most was the idea of school. Having been in the group at the Peeresses' School who studied French, I knew not a word of English. I had wanted to stay behind in Japan with my brother and graduate. But my mother had considered that it was important for girls in the years to come to learn a foreign language really well and to experience life abroad, so I had left school in mid-term to go to America.

Since the school year there began in September, it had not yet been decided which school we would attend, but whatever school we went to, we would first have to learn to speak some English. That was why I wanted to see my dear friend Masako Kabayama as soon as possible. No sooner had we arrived in San Francisco than I could hardly wait to see her again and was dying to ask her all about life in America and especially what school was like there.

I was thrilled when I found I could see her during her spring vacation. It was arranged that she should come to Washington for two weeks. But before our longed-for reunion could take place, there were several problems.

Hartridge School in New Jersey, where Masako was a student, was a strict, Catholic boarding school. Masako was the only foreign student there, and she was studying very hard. It was three hours by train from Washington, and it would not have been impossible for her to see Japanese friends, but when he sent her to study abroad, her father, Count Kabayama, had said that while she was a student he did not want her to accept any invitations from Japanese whatsoever. I imagine he felt that if she socialized with Japanese, she would not become really proficient in English. So long as she was a student in America she should cast off her Japanese self and immerse herself in the American way of life and customs.

But he made an exception in our case. However, the school laid down various difficult conditions. First of all, a teacher had to accompany her as far as Washington Station, where my mother would be expected to meet her. It was not sufficient for me to meet her alone. The school would only agree to hand her over to someone they considered responsible. So, although mother was very busy, she went with me to meet Masako and her escort, who, when she was quite satisfied that mother was indeed Madame Matsudaira, handed my friend over, on mother's assurance that she would personally come to the station again on the appointed day to return Masako to the teacher's care. Mother invited the teacher to have tea with us at the Embassy, after which the Embassy car would take her back to the station, but she declined, and went straight back. As we watched her walk away, Masako said: 'I feel like a registered parcel!'

It was the first thing Masako said at our railway station reunion. And she said it in English.

In a mere eight months, Masako could no longer speak Japanese. She could still read and write it, but the words would not come. She had not forgotten, of course – she just could not summon up the words. I was impressed with the way she had taken such pains to adapt herself and become thoroughly immersed in American life. Her father before her had gone to America to study when he was fourteen, saying it was not for himself, but for Japan. He said that Japan must become internationalized in order to take its place in the world, and so he wanted to learn about the best things in the West and come back and teach his compatriots. Therefore he was very serious about his studies.

Masako may not have been able to summon up her Japanese at first, but no sooner had she arrived at the embassy residence and relaxed, than, 'Phew! what a relief!' she exclaimed in Japanese, and we all laughed.

Judging by the teacher who brought her to Washington Station, I felt sorry for her being at such a strict school and wondered with some apprehension if that was the kind of school we would be attending. I was dying to start asking Masako all sorts of things about her life in an American school, but I was obliged to contain myself for a while longer. With her Japanese not returning much beyond 'Oh how lovely' and my English completely non-existent, it was rather difficult to communicate.

'Language is like music. If you haven't been hearing it, you get out of practise,' said Masako when she had finally begun to find her Japanese tongue again, and I think she was right. After about three days of uninhibited chatter with my sister and me, she was using Japanese and nothing else.

Hartridge School, where Masako was a student, was unusually strict for an American school. It may have been because it was Catholic, but it was more like an English school. You were not allowed to do this and you were not allowed to do that. There were so many regulations that even talkative Masako had been completely silenced. But one had to admire the way she managed – all by herself as the only foreigner.

Even though she was going to stay at the embassy, the contents of her case had had to be inspected by a teacher. She showed me what she had inside, and I was impressed by the way she had done her packing. She had not been told how to pack, it was done in her own way. She had worked out carefully what she would need and how much for the length of time she would be staying, and how big a suitcase to bring. I could see at a glance how well she had organized her things. On the top she had neatly laid the fan used in the Noh dancing she had studied since she was a child of four.

Masako visited us every vacation, and she never failed to bring her fan, although she did not necessarily dance for us. Ever since she was a primary school girl, Masako had looked stylish and dressed nicely, and on coming to America she had become even more elegant and fashionable, but it occurred to me that underlying her modern exterior she was sustained by the ancient tradition of the Japanese Noh. That, I thought, was probably the backbone that enabled her to hold her own amidst the rigours of an unfamiliar school and dormitory life.

It seems funny to speak of Masako's Japanese becoming more fluent after those three days, but when she had begun to talk freely again in Japanese, she and I stayed up all one night chattering away. 'Oh, aren't these good!' she kept saying, as we helped ourselves to pink shrimp-flavoured *sembei*, seaweed-wrapped Shinagawa Rolls, and the other varieties in the rice cracker assortment known as Edo Arare, talking incessantly. Their saltiness made us thirsty so we drank masses of green tea, and next morning we were so full we couldn't eat another thing.

The other day, Masako – now Mrs Shirasu – was reminiscing about that night and laughingly observed, 'As for what we talked about: one thing just ran into another and didn't make any sense at all!' Watching my friend so thoroughly relaxed and 'letting her hair down' in a way that she could not at boarding school made me feel carefree and happy too.

That fortnight went by in a flash, and before we knew it, Mother was taking Masako back to Washington Station and carefully handing her precious charge over to the teacher, and I had to bear the sadness of parting from Masako – who had become a 'registered parcel' again – until the summer vacation.

As the summer vacation drew near, the decision was made as to what school my sister and I would be attending, which was a relief, but while we looked forward to life at the new school, fears began to assail us regarding the English language.

THE FRIENDS SCHOOL

After a great deal of thought, our parents decided to send me to a private high school on I Street in Washington called The Friends School. My father's predecessor, Ambassador Shidehara's son had been there, and my parents had heard that it was a very good school, so after making various enquiries, they decided to send me there.

The Friends' School went from kindergarten to high school, and was co-educational. Classes in the high school were small, with only about twenty pupils. The headmaster was called Dr Thomas Sidwell, and it was a Quaker school, but there was no special religious instruction.

The fact that I could not speak English was indeed a serious trial to me. There I was in an English-speaking country and could not understand a word. For instance, although I could understand what was required for me to do in mathematics, and could write the solution correctly in my notebook, I could not put what I had done into words. How thankful I was that at least the same Arabic numerals were used worldwide!

As for English, we did not of course use language textbooks, but studied novels. Although I knew no English, I was directly faced with English literature, and found myself totally at a loss. Famous novels familiar to everyone there were quite unknown to me. I could hardly make a précis if I could not read the language the novel was written in. The only thing I could do was laboriously look up every word in a dictionary. The dictionary was never out of my hand. Whether I went home, or wherever I went, I was constantly looking up words in the dictionary. It took time. I did not dislike studying, but all that dictionary business was very hard work.

However, in spite of not being able to speak the language, never once did I experience any unpleasantness or feeling of alienation thanks to the deep emphasis placed on international friendship by the headmaster and his wife and its effect on the teachers and pupils, which made them unusually understanding and thoughtful and kind towards foreigners. The only other foreign student at that time besides my sister and me was the daughter of the Chinese Minister, who was in the class below me. We were not treated differently because we were foreigners. All the students were treated with the same warmth, and the teachers showed care and consideration in the way they disciplined us.

Homework was set daily at the Friends School, but it was not taken home. Assignments were generally finished during study periods at school. The idea was that when we got home we could play or do anything we wanted, and spend time with our families. The only students who took school books home were those with special problems, such as those who were badly behind in their studies, or foreigners like us who were not fluent in English. The students were terribly sorry for me when they saw me go out of the school gate loaded down with several books.

Latin was compulsory but I managed to be excused on the grounds that it was more important for me to concentrate on mastering English. Westerners study Latin much as we in Japan study classical Chinese, for the relation of Chinese to Japanese is similar to the relation of Latin to most European languages. Japanese is written in Chinese characters just as English, French, Italian and so forth are written in the Roman alphabet. All my friends were having a hard time with their Latin. Masako Kabayama actually liked Latin. How I admired her talent!

But while I had been excused from coping with Latin, my struggle with English continued unabated. A piano teacher had been appointed for me, but I decided that the piano was out of the question. I hardly had the time to devote myself to anything like that.

Every other month we had to take a simple test, and twice a year there was a big examination. If one got a grade of over 75 on both these examinations, one could go up one grade, but if one failed, one had to do the course over again.

Whether good or bad, the marks you received were read out in front of the whole class by the teacher without mincing matters in the slightest. In particular, those whose marks were just below the passing grade – 74, for instance – were given a thorough scolding, while the student in question would listen, looking quite unconcerned. Before I got used to this, it made me quite nervous.

When I had got to the stage where I could follow lessons in English, there was a French test in which I got the passing grade of 75. The announcement of my marks was greeted by the whole class with applause and congratulatory cheers. I thought at first that they were teasing me, since no one had applauded the girls who had got over 90 marks. I not only wondered why they had applauded, but was somewhat ashamed at what I considered a low mark, having already studied quite a bit of French at the Gakushūin – the Peeresses' School – in Tokyo. But eventually the reason became clear.

I found I was not the only student with 75 marks who was applauded. The students clapped for anyone who got 75, expressing their happiness for that person, who would beam with satisfaction and say 'Thank you' to the teacher. While it was wonderful for anyone to get over 90 marks, it was considered especially good fortune to reach 75, just over the dividing mark of failure. And as for those who got less than 75, they showed no evidence of embarrassment or despondency, and the rest of the students never showed a grain of scorn or contempt.

No one minded in the least whether anyone took three years or five years to graduate. When I discovered what a happy, cheerful atmosphere pervaded friendships and studies at the Friends School, I began to enjoy it thoroughly, and look back with nothing but nostalgia at the happy days I spent there.

Just the other day, when my lady in waiting, Mrs Shimizu, happened to be looking for something for me, she came to me and said, with a broad smile: 'Your Highness, I think you might like to see this.'

What should it be but a report card and examination paper from Friends School days! Looking at the yellowed pages, I was amazed to see that I had got 85 in English and 99 in algebra. The 85 in English pleased me much more than the 99 in Algebra, and I was transported momentarily back to those student days.

BRASS BANDS AND CHEWING GUM

My three years at the Friends School comprised the whole of my adolescence. My adolescence began and ended there, so my school memories are all the more precious to me. Those were truly happy, carefree days for me. In spite of my dictionary struggle with English, hard though it was, whenever I think of those days I find myself smiling with pleasure. And sometimes I hear in my mind the sound of an approaching circus band.

Our study hall was on the second floor, facing the road. One afternoon, when we were all quietly doing our 'prep', we began to hear the rousing music of a brass band coming closer and closer. Everyone became excited, and boys and girls sitting near the window surreptitiously craned their necks to try and see the band. It was advertising a circus. It created a stir in the study hall, making us all want to get up and look, so that we became restless and fidgety and unable to concentrate on our work. Suddenly the teacher said: 'Put down your pencils.'

We all laid our pencils down, quite sure we were going to be scolded. But to my amazement, this is what the teacher said:

'You can have ten minutes. If you want to go down to the street, you may. Or you can watch from the window, if you prefer.'

The band was just passing the school. 'Thank you!' we all shouted, and some ran down the stairs while others leaned out of the window, enjoying themselves to their heart's content. I watched from the window.

After the band had passed by, the satisfied students went back to their seats and resumed their studies with even more quiet diligence than before – and not even ten minutes had elapsed! If the teacher had ignored the students' interest and curiosity and scolded them and made them close the window, they would never have been able to resume their studies with such concentration within the brief space of ten minutes, as they did. I marvelled at the way that teacher handled the situation with such kindness and understanding, and child though I was, I could appreciate the wisdom of this kind of educational approach, and wished it could be adopted in Japan.

There was another incident that impressed me. It concerned a different teacher. This teacher was very strict about students chewing gum during class. One day, after he had come into the classroom, he sat and waited for a very long time without starting the lesson. Students began to wonder what he was waiting for, and started getting restless, but the teacher just ignored this. Then, just as the atmosphere began to change from curiosity to apprehension, he spoke:

'Will the person who is chewing gum please spit it out into that basket, immediately.'

There was no anger in his voice, but the sternness of the command caused one of the male students to spring to his feet manfully and go to the waste-basket by the platform and rid his mouth of the gum. Then to my amazement, he was followed by almost everyone else who, one by one, did the same.

But what astounded me most was that even then the teacher did not begin class. How very odd, I thought, and then the teacher said:

'Someone still has chewing gum in his mouth. Will
he please get rid of it?'

The teacher quietly waited some more, strolling back
and forth between the desks, making no attempt to
begin teaching. Not having been chewing gum myself, I
could not help feeling impatient about this waste of
time. Finally, one last student got up and deposited his
gum in the basket, and with a grin, as much as to say,
'Good, now we can begin', the teacher started class as
if nothing had happened.

There were only about two others besides myself
who had not been chewing gum. The incident taught
me a great deal. Firstly, the teacher's warmhearted
attitude. Without giving us a vigorous scolding, or
lecturing us, he treated us as responsible people and
gave us a chance to voluntarily rectify our misconduct.
As for the students, I admired their honesty and
courage in going up and getting rid of their gum when
they might have got away with it by keeping quiet. I
liked the agreeable atmosphere of good humour that
pervaded the classroom, and the warm, trusting
relationship that existed between the teachers and the
students. It was something we have never had in Japan,
either now or in the past.

I was continually amazed by one thing or another,
and in turn, I managed to provide a bit of amazement
myself. When I was a child, little girls all learned to
keep several bean bags going in the air. Taka had taught
me how to do it, but I did not consider myself
particularly adept. One day the cry went up: 'Setsuko's
a juggler!'

I had gone to the tennis-club for some afternoon
practice. During a recess, I casually threw three tennis
balls up into the air and tried the bean-bag routine. It is
not considered a particularly high-grade skill in Japan,

but my friends made a terrific fuss, and called all the other classmates over and got me to do it again for them to see. They do not play with bean-bags in America, although they have professional jugglers at circuses and vaudeville shows. They could not seem to get over the fact that I could carry off this feat with such ease. They made me do it over and over again, and when I explained that in Japan it is simply a game that all girls play, they could not stop marvelling, and came to the conclusion that all Japanese women must be jugglers and that everyone, including women and children in Japan could juggle! The fact that Westerners are not particularly dexterous may well be because they have never juggled bean bags as children.

It was my nanny, Taka, who taught me, when I was a child, in Tientsin. I even learned to sew the bags myself, out of pretty scraps of cloth, first simple bags, and finally complicated six-sided ones. One had to learn to judge just how many of the little adzuki beans to fill them with, too, for optimum performance.

Taka started me off with just one bag which she and I just threw back and forth to one another as we sat on our legs, Japanese-style, on the floor. I then had to throw the bag from one of my hands to the other. I remember how thrilled I was when I got to the stage when I could keep two bean bags going by myself, round and round with speed, from hand to hand, for one or two minutes at a time, while sitting Japanese-style on the floor. Taka could keep three going with just one hand. The next thing I had to try and do was keep three going from hand to hand without dropping one. Taka could keep four or five going with ease. There was one routine where you threw one bag up into the air, and then scooped up a certain number of others – and sometimes did various other things too –

before catching the first bag dexterously on the back of your fist as it came down.

There were special chants that went with the various routines, too. If you dropped one of the bean bags, you lost, and it was your partner's turn to see if she could keep them going longer. Taka hardly ever dropped a bean bag, and as I remember, she was a strict taskmaster, refusing to lose on purpose just to cheer me up.

Years later, when I visited Washington, an old friend asked, to my surprise: 'Do you still juggle?'

'I haven't tried lately, but I'm quite sure I could.' I replied, remembering with nostalgia the stir I had made.

Speaking of tennis balls, I have a beautiful cup I won at one of the annual school tournaments. I had played a little tennis at the Peeresses' School in Tokyo, where we used a soft ball, but although I joined the tennis club at the Friends School I had no illusions about my ability. Before I knew it, however, I found myself taking part in a tournament!

The whole school was involved, so I expected it would be quite a gala occasion, but the first round was just like an ordinary day of tennis practice. After letting us warm up for a while, the teacher simply said: 'Now we'll begin the tournament.'

The spectators were no different from the usual onlookers. I was fortunate enough to win that first day and remained in the tournament. I continued to win for the next two or three days and found myself in the semi-finals, which I also won. No-one could have been more surprised than I was to find that I would now be playing in the final! As I stood there in a daze, the girl who was to be my opponent said: 'Well, when and where shall we play?'

I looked completely blank, so she explained that we could play our match on any court we liked, whenever we wanted to.

We decided to play at a club she knew, the following Sunday, and I duly made my way there on the appointed day with a great deal of trepidation. Unlike the previous matches, the very thought that this was the final ladies singles match of the tournament made me feel nervous and tense. I arrived at the appointed place to find no-one there but my opponent – no teacher, not even an umpire. There were no spectators to encourage us and cheer – only the odd passer-by who occasionally stopped and watched. It did not feel like a tennis final at all. We had to act as our own umpire and keep score ourselves.

Perhaps my opponent never got into her stride. Whatever the reason, I won that day, too, and so I became the winner. I had won the tournament before I even realized what was happening.

Next day, when we got to the school, the two of us simply reported our score, and that was all. Was it because in America the substance is more esteemed than the form? Or was it to drive home the idea of fair play? Perhaps it was just a Friends School custom that differed from the general form taken by school tennis tournaments. Whatever the reason, for me, it is a happy memory that I have never forgotten.

At the end of term I was presented with a handsome silver cup as the ladies singles champion for that year. Not considering myself a particularly good player, I was rather more embarrassed than thrilled to see my name engraved upon it. But I was truly touched at the way everyone was so happy to see me win it, and never a word of complaint because the trophy was carried off by a foreigner. The announcement of my victory was simple. No fanfare. Just that I had won with such and such a score. I was impressed the way the school trusted the students enough to award cups based only on the students' own reporting of their scores.

## THE LINDBERGH SONG

The memory that stands out most from my Friends School days was seeing Charles A. Lindbergh whose non-stop flight across the Atlantic Ocean made him not only an American hero but a popular world figure. Not only was our school proud of his exploit but it made the school famous, for he had gone through its Primary division.

After flying the 3,630 miles from New York to Paris in thirty-three hours, Lindbergh made a triumphant return in a warship, sailing up the Potomac to Washington on 11 June 1927, where it was said that two hundred and sixty thousand people were waiting to welcome him. The crowd was ecstatic, and young women in particular went wild with frenzy over him.

President Coolidge and the citizens of Washington welcomed the young hero at a ceremony in Potomac Park, where my father was a guest, together with other diplomats. My sister and I went to the park, too, with Taka, where Lindbergh's monoplane, 'The Spirit of St Louis', was displayed. We were amazed to see how small it was. It was hard to believe that he had actually crossed the Atlantic in it. Lindbergh himself was a tall thin youth of twenty-five, who did not look at all like a hero who had just completed a great, epoch-making feat.

While Lindbergh was born in Detroit, his family had lived in Washington while his father was working at the White House and he had attended the Friends School.

After he graduated from university in mechanical engineering, he spent two years doing stunt flying, after which he got a job piloting planes carrying mail. It was during that time that he made his famous solo flight.

He must have been overcome by the unexpected ovation he received. For some time he could not remember what he was supposed to say in reply to the official welcome. He was probably busy thinking: 'Oh, mother, you'd never believe the welcome they're giving me!' Neither he nor his mother could have ever imagined in their wildest dreams the extent of the acclaim. It was not until afterwards that the public learned of the homespun background to the flight. When the story became known, I am quite sure it was their modesty and humility that appealed so tremendously to the public.

Lindbergh may have been staking his life on the venture, but he was quite confident that he could reach Paris non-stop. His mother, however, was naturally very concerned, so he promised his mother faithfully that he would do nothing rash. He assured her that should he be aware of any danger during the flight, he would land on the ocean and radio for help. 'So don't worry,' he told her. As soon as he had allayed her fears, he rushed about, hither and yon, getting people to write him letters of introduction, in spite of being very busy preparing for the flight.

As far as he was concerned, he was just an unknown mail-plane pilot, and he was afraid that if he landed in Paris, where he knew no-one, without proper letters of introduction, he might be looked on suspiciously, and he did not want that to happen. One could not fail to be moved by his sincerity and modesty. It never occurred to him that if he succeeded in his solo non-stop flight across the Atlantic Ocean the whole world would acclaim him as a hero.

His mother, too, had written a letter for him to take, stating that her son was on no suspicious errand and was an honourable mail-carrier pilot, and that she would be grateful for any kindness accorded him. After landing at an aerodrome in Paris, or elsewhere, he intended to take that letter and the others he had obtained to the American embassy and get them to vouch for his integrity.

Far from arousing suspicion, however, long before the 'Spirit of St Louis' appeared in the night sky over Paris, the aerodrome was filled with a tremendous crowd of people eager to see this brave, world hero who had accomplished such a daring feat, and his letters of introduction and his mother's affidavit proved totally unnecessary.

Nevertheless, it was hearing about those letters that caused his popularity to soar.

What appeals to me most about America is exemplified in the humility of this mother and her son and the way in which the people took this to their hearts.

Last summer, when I was at our villa in Gotemba, I frantically searched for a gramophone record. I did not think it had been destroyed in Tokyo in the fire bombing, but search as I might, I could not find it.

It was a record of a song in praise of Lindbergh. Many such records came out at that time. I bought one and brought it back with me to Japan. But when I married into the Imperial Family I was told that I should not take anything like that with me. No records of popular music or jazz. But I was sure I had hidden that record somewhere among my things, intending to listen to it secretly to bring back memories of my youth. Someone must have quietly removed it.

I am quite sure the Prince would not have minded at all about things like a record praising Lindbergh. I last listened to it at the Matsudaira house in Shibuya. I wonder what happened to that record with its memories of America and my youthful dreams.

PRINCE CHICHIBU'S VISIT

We spent an unusually quiet Christmas Eve in 1926 on account of the Emperor Taishō's grave illness. His Majesty died the following day. The embassy flag was draped in mournful black, and father received condolences from the representatives of the various nations. We all went into mourning and were filled with thoughts of our grieving homeland far away. My mother wept as she thought of the dear lady she would now have to call the Empress Dowager, and regretted not being there to attend upon Her Majesty. My eyes, too, filled with tears as I thought of how kindly the Empress Dowager had spoken to me, and remembered how affectionately the late Emperor had watched from the upstairs window of the Imperial villa in Nikko as Prince Sumi engaged in a bit of fun with my sister and me in the garden below.

In addition to the sadness, the whole embassy became caught up in a bustle of activity which affected all of us. His Imperial Highness, Yasuhito, Prince Chichibu was arriving in Washington on the 29th and would be staying overnight at the embassy residence.

The Japanese Foreign Ministry had earlier informed my father that Prince Chichibu, then studying in London, would be returning to Japan via the United States to the bedside of his ailing father, the Emperor, but even so it was rather sudden, and also there was the fact that the Emperor's death had changed the status of the Prince. Whereas he had been the second son of the sovereign, he was now first in the line of succession to the throne, and for the embassy, who would be receiving him, the tension mounted.

It was impossible at that late date to arrange for the Prince to stay elsewhere in view of his higher position, so it was decided that the whole of the second floor, where the best bedroom was, would be made available to the Prince and his attendants, which meant that we, as a family, would have to move to the third floor.

My father went to New York the day before the Prince was due to arrive and was at the wharf to meet him together with three hundred Japanese residents, so mother was left in sole charge and earnestly implored the three of us, over and over again, to be well-behaved.

'We are having a very important guest indeed, so do please try not to cause any trouble.'

Mother knew that whenever there was a lively gathering below, curiosity would get the better of us, and we would peer down from the top of the stairs. It was not surprising on my small brother's part, but since my sister and I were also in the habit of turning out the lights and peeking, I suppose she was worried. 'You definitely are not to do that', she told us, having lined the three of us up together. thinking about it now, I realize that I was still a child in those days.

The Prince spent one night at the Plaza Hotel in New York and then came on to Washington, where he was welcomed at Central Station by Secretary of State Frank Billings Kellogg.

As the time approached for His Imperial Highness to arrive at the embassy residence, all the staff – my mother, we children, and Taka – lined up in the entrance hall, dressed in mourning. Being a high school student I did not possess anything suitable, so a black dress had to be made for me in a hurry. It was the first time I had ever worn a black silk dress, and I still remember the feel of the fabric, and how grown-up I felt.

The car finally drew up, and we all bowed as the Prince got out, and he, in turn, nodded in greeting as my father led him inside, followed by his entourage.

After that, we three children were sent up to the third floor. My sister and I, however, had been entrusted with the duty of serving tea and refreshments to His Highness while he relaxed after having taken a bath, so we remained on tenterhooks. We kept thinking how awful it would be if we dropped a teacup, or spilled some of the *o-shiruko*. My mother had been told the His Highness had a sweet tooth, so she had been busy all morning preparing the sweet *azuki*-bean drink, as well as *sushi*, for she thought these homely Japanese dishes might be a comfort to the bereaved Prince.

Mother sent for us when it was time, and after my sister and I had taken the tea, *sushi* and *o-shiruko*, I being the eldest, stayed behind to serve them. The Prince seemed to enjoy the hot, thick bean drink, for he asked for a second helping. As I handed it to him, he enquired as to what school I went to, and listened with interest as I told him various things about the Friends School. He wanted to know what I was studying, and what sports I participated in. I remember explaining that although I had at first had difficulty learning English, it was a wonderful school, and I was now enjoying my studies quite a lot.

At the Palace in Tokyo and on the train to Izu I had

only been able to bow to the Prince, but this time it was just the two of us, and although I was answering the Prince's questions, I was able for the first time to express my own opinions and ideas. I was in a sort of daze while the conversation was going on, and when I got downstairs I found myself trembling with excitement.

That is why I cannot remember very much about that first conversation with the Prince, but one thing was certain, His Highness seemed quite a different person to me then from the way he had appeared to me before. It may have been something to do with the year-and-a-half he had spent studying in London, but I found him as easy to get along with as any ordinary young man.Apart from the *o-shiruko* and *sushi*, mother saw that His Highness was provided with everything else, so I only had that very brief conversation with the Prince.

On account of the late Emperor's death, no large dinner party was held. Dinner was informal, with some of the embassy staff and members of the Prince's suite, but we children were not included. Taka brought our food up to the third floor.

Next day, accompanied by my father, the Prince laid a wreath at the Tomb of the Unknown Soldier in Arlington, then after visiting the Lincoln Memorial and George Washington's home, he paid a courtesy call on President Coolidge at the White House. The President seemed touched that the twenty-four-year-old Prince should take the time to call on him on his sad homeward journey, and he put his arms around the Prince's shoulders with genuine compassion, as if he were his own son, and led him into his office for a thirty-minute private chat.

The Prince returned to the embassy residence for a

rest, after which he addressed a few words of thanks to the embassy staff and ourselves before setting off homeward via Chicago and San Francisco.

While mother, together with the embassy staff, could not help but feel a certain relief after the inevitable strain of an Imperial visit, all of them, especially my mother, had tears in their eyes at the thought of his father, the late Emperor's sad lying-in-state that awaited our recent guest, imagining what his emotions must be.

The Prince, then a lieutenant in the Infantry, had arrived in London on 7 July 1925, to study in England. He was to enter Oxford University the following year, in October, and until that time was busily learning English as well as indulging in various sports, climbing mountains in Switzerland, going to the cinema, shopping, and generally enjoying himself living the life of an ordinary citizen. He had been hoping to spend at least a year at Oxford, studying modern British History, Politics, and Economics, but had only been attending lectures for two months when, after the first term, during the Christmas vacation, he was called home to Japan because of his father's illness.

Nowadays, it would take only a few hours by air, but at that time, the Prince, impatient though he was to be with his critically-ill father, had to cover the six thousand miles from London to Japan by ocean liner and train. The embassy arranged for the Prince to travel via America as it was the shortest feasible route, and the cable announcing the Emperor's death reached him in mid-Atlantic, only three days after his ship, the '*Majestic*', had sailed from England.

Prince Chichibu finally reached Yokohama on 17 January 1927. He went immediately to the Palace, where he paid his respects to the late Emperor as he lay in state, and called upon the Empress Dowager. He then called upon the new Emperor and Empress at the Akasaka Detached Palace.

On 20 January, he visited the Palace again, as the representative of Emperor Hirohito, to report his succession to the spirit of the late Emperor, who would henceforth be known, according to custom, by his reign name as Emperor Taishō. It was the Prince's first duty as the next in line to the throne. That day, his aide-de-camp was Lt. Colonel Masaharu Honma – later Commander-in-Chief of the Philippines in World War II, who was held responsible for the Bataan Death March and received the death penalty at the war crimes trial in Manila. He was a good, kind, faithful, man. I will write more about him later.

The Prince had left Oxford expecting it to be only a temporary absence while his father, the Emperor, was ill. However, on becoming the first in line to the throne, he had to abandon his cherished dream of returning to the university.

As for me, I knew nothing of all this – indeed, there was no reason why I should know – and I worked hard at my lessons every day. I was beginning to enjoy my studies immensely, although I had no particular ambition to establish myself as a scholar. I found that one did not have to be brilliant, but that just by diligently amassing bits of knowledge, vistas opened out that one could not see before, and it gave a great sense of fulfilment. After graduating from high school, I secretly thought about going on to study further.

WALTZING WITH DADDY

I saw far more of my father in America than anywhere else, and so my memories of him are closely bound up with my adolescence. I have few memories of him as a child, for although we lived in the same house, the things children do and think are so far removed from the adult world that the lives of one's parents tend to make little impression. Besides, my father was an extremely busy man. After my marriage into the Imperial Family, there was no possiblity for a normal father-daughter relationship. The Imperial Household was not like it is today, and so as far as I can remember, I hardly ever saw anybody much from outside the Imperial circle. It was more or less the same as regards my mother. I probably remember my father more, since it was he who usually scolded me.

My three years in America are precious to me, not only as the years of my adolescence, but as a time spent with my family. My father had a little free time, which he never had in Japan, and was able to spend it with his family. I am only sorry my elder brother was not there too.

Among the scoldings I received from my father, I particularly remember the time my sister and I collapsed with laughter just as a guest had departed. A member of the embassy staff had come to see father on some urgent business just before Sunday lunch and we asked him to join us for the family meal. Something or other had struck us as being funny and my sister and I were in the middle of a fit of the giggles when we were called to come down for lunch. We were at that age when one could start giggling at the drop of a chopstick and we had a hard time trying to control ourselves as we went downstairs to the dining-room.

Our guest was someone we knew, but it would never have done to laugh in his presence, so we ate with eyes lowered, avoiding looking at one another in a desperate attempt to prevent our laughter from break-ing out anew. Somehow we managed to get through the meal and fortunately, the guest left straight away, but it was all my sister and I could do to control ourselves as we all saw him to the door, and it was hardly closed when we erupted simultaneously in a loud burst of laughter.

My father's anger was like thunder.

'It's frightfully rude to laugh out loud when you've just seen someone off and you're not sure they're out of earshot! You may not be laughing at them, but they'll think you are. It's even inadmissable in a small child, and you're certainly old enough to know better.'

His angry blast extinguished our convulsions at once, and made us realize what a dreadful thing we had done. To this day, I have not the slightest idea what it could have been that struck us as being so hilarious.

Another occasion concerns my father's inordinate sensitivity to smells. He did not smoke, and he even objected to the smell of a packet of cigarettes in the pocket of his secretary sitting next to him in the car.

He was very particular about smells in the house when we were entertaining. We often served *sukiyaki* in Washington – an aroma that tends to linger. Father was very fond of *sukiyaki*, but as soon as the meal was over, he would insist that the windows were opened wide to get rid of the smell, and decreed that this and other similar dishes cooked on the table not be served for at least two days beforehand whenever we were going to have a party, and made quite sure the rooms had been well aired and the curtains shaken out. He maintained it was bad manners to receive guests in any but fresh-smelling rooms, and that unfamiliar cooking odours were apt to be particularly unwelcome to people of another country. I still follow my father's custom from those Washington days and never fail to

open the windows after serving one-pot cook-it-
yourself meals.

We once were having a Japanese-style dinner party at
the embassy, and everything was ready when father
came into the dining-room and complained of a funny
smell. It was just as the guests were beginning to arrive,
and we all sniffed hard to find out what it was, when
daddy called out, 'This is it!' and what should it turn
out to be but glue that had gone stale in the envelopes
containing the pairs of disposable chopsticks! I do not
remember what we did about it.

With such a sensitive nose it is not surprising that my
father was somewhat finicky about what he ate. The
only fruit he would eat was a certain variety of
persimmon from Aizu. He had a stern side to him,
but called us by affectionate pet-names when he was in
a good mood. I was Set-chan and my sister Masako was
either Ma-chan or Mak-ko, while our little brother Jiro,
whom he adored, was just Ji.

Father was quite plump when we were in Washington, but he loved to waltz, and even when he came
home tired after playing golf, he would completely
revive in the evening when he heard us playing the
gramophone and come and ask us to put on the 'The
Blue Danube' or 'The Merry Widow' and ask me or my
sister to dance with him. Giggling, we would meekly
oblige. He and Mother used to dance a lot together
when they were younger, but we were his dancing
partners in Washington. He loved Caruso, and often
treated us children to a rendition of an aria from *La
Traviata*.

At New Year, we always entertained the Japanese
staff and their families with traditional New Year food,
after which there would be games. In the evening there
would be cards and mahjong. Father preferred billiards,

of which he was very fond. The Naval Attaché at the time was Isoroku Yamamoto. He was a marvellous dancer, and when he played cards and mahjong, he invariably won. He had a very keen sixth sense, or perhaps it was luck. Whenever we played a game where we drew up sides, everyone wanted to be on his team.

In April, 1943, when the war was going badly for us, I heard that Fleet Commander-in-Chief Admiral Yamamoto's plane had crashed and that he was missing. I remember thinking: 'This is the end. Japan's going to lose the war. His special luck has finally run out. We're bound to lose now.' I can say it now. I could not say that to anyone then.

THE FUROSHIKI AND THE HOLE-IN-ONE

Although daddy had a stern side, he was at heart a doting father and was, surprisingly, more lenient than mother. If there was something we wanted to do, such as an opera we wanted very much to see in New York, we would approach him when he was in a good mood and there was a very good chance that he would take us. There was no use wheedling him if he was tired and irritable after a hard day's work. At times like that, we would do things for him, like massaging his shoulders, or putting on his favourite Caruso record. It was always worth the effort, and the end result as likely as not would be a family visit to the opera, which daddy enjoyed too.

My sister was the most successful wheedler. She was rather frail, and for quite a few years until the birth of our little brother she had been the baby – and daddy's pet. So when I did not have her help, it was somewhat harder to get my way on my own. I was desperately anxious to go to the Davis Cup match in New York. I had not been allowed to go the year before, and this year I was determined to see it. I was very keen on tennis and the match I wanted to see was an important one between Japan and America. There were some very good players on the Japanese team in those days, such as Hisako Kajikawa, and Fumiko Tamura, as well as male tennis stars like Shimizu, Harada and Asabuki. It was the heyday of Japanese tennis.

My father was too busy to take me, and at first he would not hear of my going alone, but after a great deal of coaxing – which I had to do on my own, since my sister was not interested in sports and gave me no support – he finally gave in, to my great joy.

The fact that we happened to be staying in a place not far from New York helped. That summer, instead of going to a resort, as usual, we took a house near New York, since it was convenient for my father's work and there were many Japanese living there. There were tennis-courts nearby where I could practise every day, and it was a tremendous thrill being able to attend the Davis Cup matches.

While he was in America, my father used to play golf every week. He even played the day of the Lindbergh Reception after the ceremony in Potomac Park was over – and something awfully funny happened. Mother told us about it, trying hard to control her laughter. Daddy himself never mentioned the incident to us, I suppose because he was not sure whether to be proud of his feat, or the opposite. Apparently, his first drive hit something not far from the hole and bounced out of sight. The three players were carrying their own bags so none of them saw where the ball had gone. After they had all searched high and low, it was finally discovered down in the hole itself. Thinking nothing of it, one of them lifted out the ball with the comment, 'So that's where it was hiding!', when a group of students arrived from behind, exclaiming: 'What a magnificent hole-in-one!'

It had not occurred to my father at all. After all, it was just a fluke. And yet, to all intents and purposes it was indeed a hole-in-one!

Another amusing episode concerns Taka. She had been with us for so long that it did not bother us the way she dressed while in America. She had her own style. We had accepted the fact long ago that Taka had her own way of doing things, so what she wore in America did not bother us much. At first glance it was difficult to tell whether it was a kimono or a dress. We were also used to her always insisting on taking her daughter Chie with her whenever she went shopping. But one thing irritated me. It was the fact that she made no effort whatsoever to learn English. I considered her refusal to do so downright discourteous to America.

'Taka', I would say, 'since you are lucky enough to be here, I think the least you might do is learn enough English to be able to go shopping by yourself and find your way around.'

'I dislike the English language', she would reply, obstinately.

We frequently quarrelled about it.

Taka was fond of the Japanese classics, and spent any free time she had reading. That was all very well, but she was living in America, so even if she could not read English I felt she should at least *look* at a local newspaper once in a while. I wanted her to get the feel of America, and try to familiarize herself with the country. But Taka was stubborn, and flatly refused to do so. I was stubborn, too, and wanted so much for her to get to know America even just a little.

'Oh, do leave poor Taka alone,' said Masako Kabayama once when she was visiting us during the winter vacation. 'She's a bit eccentric, I know, but it's not that she's just being awkward. It's her nature. She's being true to herself, and I think that's wonderful. And moreover, she gets along perfectly well inside the embassy.'

Masako's wisdom as an impartial observer gave me much to think about. But a few days later, it was Masako's turn to be embarrassed by Taka. So much so that she actually turned tail and fled. We were all shopping together for Christmas-tree ornaments, when Taka, who was conspicuous enough as it was, deliberately drew out of her bosom a commodious cotton *furoshiki* – traditional dark green, patterned all over with white arabesques – and shaking out the enormous square wrapping cloth she spread it out right there in the middle of the store thronged with shoppers, who started to crowd round with curiosity.

'Oh no!' cried Masako, and rushed out of the store, while my sister and I followed close behind. There was no doubt that the *furoshiki* was an immensely practical way to deal with all the bits and pieces we had bought. Paying no attention to the people around her, Taka wrapped all our Christmas shopping in the cloth square and heaving the bundle onto her shoulders came towards us, leaving Chie to settle up. Taka's courage of her convictions made her completely oblivious to the curious looks she attracted. Hers was not mindless eccentricity. It was bred of education and culture. It was just Taka's way, and as I watched her carrying that large bundle with dignity and self-composure I found myself filled with admiration.

Masako, who had shared this and so many more memories with me, finally completed her studies and returned to Japan. I no longer had her company at holidays to look forward to but I enjoyed my studies more and more and my days were replete with fulfilment.

THE EMISSARY

Washington is a beautiful city, often likened to one great park. In October, 1927, just as the trees in Potomac Park and The Mall and those lining the roads that radiate from the Capitol were becoming more and more resplendent in their autumn colours, we heard that Count Kabayama was to visit us at the embassy. He was said to be on urgent, though unspecified business, and had already left Japan when father received a cable from the Foreign Ministry apprising us of his imminent arrival. I imagined it must be something that had come up suddenly, or Masako would surely have mentioned it in her recent letter to me. But I did not give it as much thought as my parents did, since it was no doubt some government or diplomatic business unlikely to concern me. I eagerly looked forward to his visit, however, since he would bring news of Masako.

Count Kabayama was a Vice Admiral in the Navy and also, as I remember, a Director of an iron works as well as being a Member of the House of Peers. Countess Kabayama's father – Masako's maternal grandfather – Count Kawamura, one time Secretary of State for the Navy and former Privy Councillor, had, at the instigation of Emperor Meiji, acted as foster father to Emperor Shōwa and his brother Prince Chichibu from soon after their birth until they were three and two respectively. When Count Kawamura died, the two Imperial grandsons moved to a temporary residence in the Aoyama Palace grounds.

Count Kabayama duly arrived, bringing me a gift from Masako. He and my parents were still talking downstairs when I decided to go to bed after having studied until quite late, and I noticed that the downstairs lights were still on when I woke up briefly in the middle of the night. I wondered if the Count's important business had anything to do with some sort of worrisome complications that might have arisen over the recent succession of Emperor Hirohito to the throne. But I did not imagine it was anything I needed to worry about, although I did think it was rather strange that my mother should be taking part the whole time in the conversation. She had never remained before when political discussions were going on.

When I came home from school the following afternoon, they were still at it, and moreover, went on talking until midnight. My parents never said anything to me, but I noticed my father looked sombre, and my mother's face was drawn. It seemed as if it must be something very worrying for it to cast a gloom over the whole house. Even Taka was strangely quiet and her stern features were more sullen than usual and she seemed ill at ease. I came to the conclusion it could not be anything political, and feared that Count Kabayama had brought some awful news connected with our family. My sister Masako, too, seem to sense that something was wrong, but neither of us spoke of it to the other, as there was obviously little we could do, whatever it was. When we came home from school on the third day, we found that Count Kabayama had left. I regretted not having known he was leaving, for I should have liked to have had a letter and gift ready for him to take back to Masako. The tension in the house seemed to have lifted, so I thought the problem must have been resolved, which was a great relief.

But no sooner had he arrived back in Japan than we learned that Count Kabayama was on his way back to Washington. This really must be something very serious, I thought. Nevertheless, neither Masako nor I, nor even Taka, dared ask any questions, for there seemed to be an impenetrable and invisible wall between us and our parents.

Count Kabayama was stony faced when he arrived, and began conferring with my parents straight away, and they talked until late that night. Next day, he sent for me, and spoke to me alone. He told me that this time he had come as the personal emissary of the Empress Dowager to persuade me, Setsuko Matsudaira, to agree to become Her Imperial Highness Princess Yasuhito Chichibu. He had been charged by Her Majesty to obtain without fail the consent of both the parents and the daughter herself.

I was overwhelmed. I was speechless. My head went quite blank, and I sat there stiff and tense, like a stone.

'When I was here before,' said the Count,' I was given a very definite refusal by your parents, who would not even allow me to ask you myself. On returning to Japan, I explained fully to Her Majesty your parents' reasons for their decision. But Her Majesty is very strong-willed. I am here because she reprimanded me for not having succeeded. Your parents feel that as loyal subjects they can no longer continue to disobey Her Majesty, and so they have given me permission to speak to you myself.'

So 'Uncle' Kabayama – who used to call me by the affectionate diminutive 'Set-chan' when I visited them at their country villa in Gotemba in my primary school days – had been saddled with the painful task, as emissary of the Empress Dowager, of being obliged to prevail over his friends and their daughter against their will!

Count Kabayama gave me the details of my parents' original reply to Her Majesty. My father had said that while he felt greatly honoured, he felt unworthy and that it was his duty as Her Majesty's loyal subject to decline the offer. The gist of my father's reply is a follows:

'The consort of Prince Chichibu, the Heir to the Throne, should be someone of suitable rank and ability. My daughter Setsuko has been brought up as a perfectly ordinary girl and is not capable of filling that position. Furthermore, not only am I, Tsuneo Matsudaira, now a commoner, but in addition, Setsuko's grandfather – for whatever the exigencies of the Imperial army were at the time of the Restoration – was stigmatized as a rebel. It would be inadmissible, therefore, for his granddaughter to become the consort of the heir to the throne. I beg you to consider the Aizu connection.'

My mother, too, apparently, had demurred most vehemently, saying, 'Setsuko is just an average, ordinary girl, quite natural and unrestrained, who has never been taught any of the refinements that would prepare her for life at Court.'

My mother having been a lady-in-waiting to the Empress Dowager knew what she was talking about, so when she firmly declared that I was not at all the sort of girl who could suitably discharge the responsibilities of a princess, Count Kabayama had given up trying to pursue the matter any further.

'As you yourself well know,' my mother had reiterated, 'Setsuko has never had any training in manners and etiquette, and is just a plain, ordinary girl with no social graces at all.'

So those discussions I had wondered about that had lasted until the early hours of the morning had been a long verbal battle in which my father and mother had kept on resisting along these lines and Count Kabayama had tried hard to break their arguments down.

When the Count reported his failure to the Empress Dowager, she was greatly displeased and said: 'Well, in that case I shall just have to send somebody else.'

So back he had come, and I heard later that he had made up his mind while on board the ship never to set foot on Japanese soil again unless it be with a positive answer. When my parents heard of his desperate decision, they agonized over it again, and finally said: 'As parents of a girl who is not qualified to become the consort of the heir to the throne, propriety obliged us to decline the offer, but if Her Majesty's heart is so set upon it, it would surely be discourteous on our part to continue to refuse.'

It was as if my parents had been a breakwater which was suddenly taken away, leaving me about to be engulfed unexpectedly by an immense ocean wave. I had not the slightest idea what to say.

'It is surely incumbent upon me to refuse,' I stammered, 'for I have never been taught how to behave in such a position. Why, it seems quite preposterous that someone like myself should marry into the Imperial Family. There are so many other Japanese girls. . . . Why me? I am not even a member of the nobility, and only managed to get into the Peeresses' School by passing the special examinations. I must certainly refuse.'

I threw at him every reason I could think of to get myself out of the predicament I found myself in. I was not merely unhappy, I was frantic.

'Why me? I'm just not cut out to be a princess, so why me?'

I refused to go to school. I refused to eat. I just stayed in my room and cried my eyes out after leaving the matter in the Count's hands. It could not have been easy for my parents, either, for they stood at the parting of the ways with their daughter.

Guessing how weary the Count must be, Mother offered to have Taka try to persuade me. My nanny having brought me up with such tender care from infancy, Mother thought Taka and I would be able to discuss the matter more easily. But I was torn with anguish at the thought of having to become an Imperial princess so suddenly, with no preparation whatever, after having lived the life of an ordinary girl until the age of eighteen. I did not see how I could manage it. Moreover, it was unprecedented. Count Kabayama had said the Empress Dowager would guide me in everything to do with the Court, and that I need not worry, but it seemed to me that more was at stake than just learning rules – I sensed that the Imperial Family lived in a completely different dimension from ordinary people. Even Taka did not seem to understand this. Or so I thought. But when I confronted her with it, instead of refuting my theory with vigour as she usually did, she said in a choked voice:

'I know exactly how you feel. So does His Lordship; and so does Madam. They are very, very well aware of it indeed. That is why they both look so drawn.'

And she went on: 'The Empress Dowager has sent Count Kabayama here twice. Her Majesty obviously wishes it fervently. So I really think there is nothing you can do but make up your mind to accept.'

Taka also said it would set my parents' minds at rest if I did.

I stopped crying and just sat there, curiously drained of all emotion, and quietly, in my mind – just as if I were turning the pages of a photograph album – I pictured the day at the Imperial villa in Nikko, the time we met Prince Chichibu in the train to Izu, and the time the Prince asked me about my school when he stayed overnight at the embassy.

Why should those images have come into my thoughts just then, when I was in such a desperate frame of mind, driven into a corner as it were and being obliged to say 'yes' just because my parents had already given their agreement?

Looking back now, I think it must have been a desperate attempt to try and imagine what it would be like living in that world that seemed so far apart from my own.

'Taka,' I said, 'if I become a member of the Imperial Family I shan't be able to see much of my sister and my brothers any more, shall I? And it won't be the same any more between mummy and daddy and me, either, will it? It'll be awful.'

There was one more thing on my mind. 'And Taka, it isn't going to affect just me. As relatives of a princess, they won't be at liberty any longer to live as they please, will they?'

Tears suddenly began trickling down Taka's cheeks. When she had dried them, she said, 'No, but they possess the Aizu spirit.'

At the word 'Aizu' I suddenly thought of that night in Aoyama when my father had scolded me for being scared as I watched him gazing so intently at his drawn sword. And as I did so, a strength rose up within me which presently formed itself into the decision to do as the Empress Dowager wished. And I seemed to see the two characters 'Ai-zu' shining through the black, lowering clouds and illuminating the path for me to take.

After thinking it through once more, I said, as I remember, 'I will do as Her Majesty wishes. Please tell Uncle Kabayama and daddy and mummy.' It was Taka who began to cry. I remained quite calm and collected.

I had thought, agonized, and cried myself dry. Now that my mind was made up I would reflect and cogitate no more. Since I had no idea what my future life would be like, I resolved not to be apprehensive, or to fret. I decided to live in the present, to make the most of every day. That would prepare me best for the future. That was the conclusion I finally arrived at.

But I have to admit I cried the whole night after finally making my decision. I heard years later from my elder brother's wife that Taka had confided to her: 'I am not exaggerating: her bath-towel was absolutely soaked with tears, and the poor child's face was swollen with crying.' And Masako – by that time Mrs Shirasu – told me long after that how her father, Count Kabayama, had returned home totally exhausted, saying: 'I was almost at the end of my tether. I didn't get any sleep for three nights, Set-chan was so damned obstinate.'

Looking back over my life, I have come to the conclusion that there are two kinds of grief: one that you can laugh about in retrospect, and another – like that occasioned by the loss of my husband, the late Prince – that grows deeper and harder to bear as the years go by.

CHAPTER FOUR

# *Until My Wedding Day*

THE MEMORY BOOK

*T*he die was cast, and I had resolved to live each day to the fullest, so I threw myself into my studies. My graduation from the Friends School was but half a year away, in June. I had wanted to go on to university and study science, but there was no hope now of staying on in America for further study after my father's tour of duty was over, so I would have to make the most of the precious time left to me of my student days.

Neither would it be long before I was separated from my family by an immense social chasm, so I wanted each day that was left to be as happy as possible so I could cherish them in my mind. I tried not to let this show, and made a great effort to act as I always had.

But nevertheless, the atmosphere at home was not the same as it had been before. My father and mother spoke less, and even when daddy joined my sister and me when we were listening to records, he was not as

*64*

animated as he used to be, and I sensed a strange restraint. Even when I persuaded him to dance with me, he seemed ill at ease.

While he presented an imposing figure on the world diplomatic stage, my father was shy and awkward by nature, and try as he might to act as though nothing had changed I could see that he was nervous in my presence, and it made me want to cry. I had heard that fathers become very sad when their daughters leave to be married, so I tried especially hard to be cheerful for his sake, and not to look dispirited.

At the end of 1927, Taka left for Japan, charged by my father to make all the necessary preparations for the wedding. Her daughter Chie returned with her, leaving the school she was attending. She had similarly interrupted her English Literature studies at Aoyama Gakuin when she came to America with us. They spent New Year's Day, 1928, on the train crossing America, and Taka wrote in her diary: 'My errand seems weightier than the Rocky Mountains.'

Although my betrothal to Prince Chichibu was still unofficial, news of it leaked out and appeared in the American press, which led to it becoming big news in Japan. Facts were garbled, as often happens, and it was made to look as if there had been a romance between the Prince and me. Unkind things were written too, and refutations printed, but I was not told about any of this at the time.

On 13 January 1928, while Taka was still crossing the Pacific, I was officially entered – as his niece – in the family register of my uncle Viscount Morio Matsudaira, for the former Imperial House Act stipulated that princes and princesses of the blood might marry only members of royalty or the nobility.

Then, on 18 January, notice was conveyed to the

House of Matsudaira by the Imperial Household Minister as follows:

'Imperial sanction is hereby granted for the matrimonial alliance of His Imperial Highness Prince Yasuhito to Setsuko, niece of Viscount Morio Matsudaira, Senior Grade of the Fourth Court Rank, Third Order of Merit Fifth Class.'

An official announcement was made simultaneously by the Imperial Household.

Having no royalty or nobility of their own, the Americans are greatly attracted by it, and the fact that the Japanese Ambassador's daughter, a student at one of their schools, was about to become a princess caused a furore among the media. Thankfully, my mother took care of the numerous newspapers and magazine people who came wanting interviews. Japanese reporters were particularly tiresome.

Everyone congratulated me at school but were very considerate and allowed me to go about my studies in peace like an ordinary student, just as before.

Taka and her daughter arrived in Yokohama at dawn on 21 January and were besieged by the press in spite of the early hour.

'Look here, I'm not the one who's getting married', Taka is said to have declared indignantly. When I heard about it I could not help laughing. It was so like her. But judging by later press cuttings, she obviously learned how to deal with them splendidly. Always prefacing her comments by an assurance that she was being quite impartial, in spite of having brought me up, she was so profuse in praise about my character and personality and even my scholastic ability that reading it now makes me blush. She was, however, realistic and objective about my daily life and categorically refuted the myth of a romance between the Prince and me.

Until our return home in the middle of June 1928, Taka worked tirelessly on the preparations for my wedding, with both public and private help and advice of my uncle and aunt and others such as Itsuko, Princess Nashimoto, my Nabeshima grandparents, and Count Kabayama.

Princess Nashimoto, who was my mother's elder sister, and my cousin, her daughter Masako, Princess Li, were able to give many a tip from their experience, which helped my aunt and Taka considerably. Taka also had to make arrangements for our mansion in Tokyo's Shibuya ward to be renovated in time for our return, as well as dealing with media harassment. The extent of Taka's anxiety and concern is evident in the entry in her diary in which she tells of how she kept a dagger tucked into her *obi* at all times, and whenever anything happened, she placed her hand upon it for reassurance.

However, the entry for 26 April reads 'Today's evening paper joyfully announced Lady Setsuko's arrival date and the date set for the official exchange of betrothal gifts. It included happy comments from many well-meaning citizens. As I think of her ship as it sets sail with fair spring winds, I am grateful. . . .'

Taka was obviously relieved to read that I had millions of people on my side.

Meanwhile, I had many things to think about as my 18 May graduation approached. After graduation was over, I was to leave Washington for Japan on 1 June. I might never see my teachers and friends again, and wanting something to remember them by I went around asking each of them to write something in my memory book.

But their reaction was curious. In spite of having been such good friends, no-one seemed to want to do so. A few grinned sheepishly and merely signed their names. I was very disappointed. A few days before graduation, however, there was to be a talk of some sort and we all gathered in the assembly hall, where after it was announced that my sister and I would be leaving for Japan, to our surprise we each received a gift. And what should mine turn out to be but a magnificent, large, handsomely-bound, specially-produced memory book!

Not only did it contain signatures, but there was a photograph of the headmaster and his wife and all the teachers, as well as group photographs and close-ups of the students, and all sorts of nostalgic snapshots. And to cap it all, my teachers and schoolmates had written messages of warmth and friendship, wishing me happiness in my future life as a princess – messages brimming over with encouragement and inspiration.

I was overwhelmed. I hardly knew what to say. 'Thank you so much. I shall treasure this all my life.' That was about all I could manage.

But alas, the memory book is no more. It was reduced to ashes in the fire bombing during the war, together with the palace we lived in. Only my graduation certificate, in its thin leather case, survived. Although it had been in a safe, it was badly shrivelled by the heat – but it proves that I am a graduate of the Friends School.

On the night of 18 May 1928, when the graduation took place, little did anyone imagine there would be a horrible war. There were fourteen of us graduating – seven boys and seven girls – and we sat in a row on the stage in the assembly hall, the boys in tuxedos and the girls in white formals carrying bouquets of crimson roses. After congratulating us and bidding us farewell, the headmaster presented us each in turn, with a final benediction, our parchment certificate tied with a maroon and gray ribbon – the school colours.

On the platform that day, the Rising Sun was displayed in my honour beside the Stars and Stripes, which the headmaster presented to me in his warm thoughtfulness. I still remember how deeply touched I was.

As they carried away their graduation certificates – their passports to the future – I wondered what hopes and dreams my classmates carried with them as they spread their wings and flew away out into the world. As for me, as I set off on the path of my destiny, I vowed to myself that I would follow it faithfully and do my very best.

RIGHT AND PROPER

The days following my graduation were busy with preparations to leave Washington for good, for in addition to having obtained leave of absence on account of my wedding, my father had been designated ambassador to Great Britain. The post of ambassador to the Court of St James is considered the diplomatic pinnacle, but my father did not seem happy about it at all.

Taka told me that it had been for two reasons that he had persisted so long in opposing the Empress Dowager's wish for me to marry her son. The fact that he considered me quite unsuitable had been the prime consideration, but in addition to that, he did not want advancement in his career by virtue of his daughter being a member of the Imperial Family.

'He is that sort of man,' she said. 'When they wanted to make His Lordship a member of the present nobility, the reason he renounced the headship of the family and the title in favour of Master Morio was because he felt, as a member of the former Aizu clan, that it would be unfair to those clan members whose own chances of advancement had been ruined.'

My father had climbed the rungs of the diplomatic ladder by his own efforts alone, as an ordinary person, with no influential backing, so having reached the position of ambassador extraordinary and plenipotentiary in Washington, it would seem only natural that his next appointment would be to the prestigious London post, so it saddened me to think that he should have misgivings. My heart ached to think that becoming an Imperial in-law might have the effect of changing the personality of my dear father – so strict but so magnanimous, and with such an endearing childlike quality.

One day not long before we left Washington, my father called me to him, saying he would like to have a nice quiet chat with me since it might be hard to find time to do so once we were back in Japan.

'I want you to know', he said, 'how happy I am that you have turned out to be the kind of girl I had always hoped you would be. I wanted you to grow up just an ordinary girl who was good and upright – someone who could be counted on to do what is right and proper in any situation. You will need that more than ever now. You must not just make do and pretend, hoping it will look right. You must know your place, and always be aware of your position. A student, for example, acts like a student, and does whatever is required in that capacity. Since fate has decreed this for you, put your heart and soul into doing the very best you can.'

Daddy pointed out that suddenly entering Court life like this out of the blue, there were bound to be many things I would not know how to do, so it would require great dilligence on my part. He warned me against pretence and muddling through, for I would not be able to keep it up. If I tried my very best with wholehearted sincerity and then failed, there would be nothing to be ashamed of. It would be quite different from failure for lack of effort.

'And as I'm sure you already know,' he added, 'if you do not think of effort as a trial and tribulation but try to gain satisfaction from it, and even joy, you will be able to continue that effort all your life. Above all, put sincerity first.'

My father spoke with deliberate calm, holding in check the multitude of thoughts crowding his heart. As for me, his manner of speech gave me a wrench. My sister had told me that on the day of the official announcement of my betrothal, daddy had said to her and our brother: 'We mustn't think of Setsuko any more as one of us. We must think of her as having been entrusted to our care by His Imperial Highness,' so I realized that his use of the formal rather than the familiar 'you' in speaking to me now had been his way of distancing father from daughter. But his smile, and the warmth that I could feel told me my father had not changed. I loved him so much and wanted to throw my arms about his neck as I used to do as a child, but I also realized that now that I had made the decision to marry into the Imperial Family I would have to move away step by step from those I loved.

It was not long, however, before our tête-à-tête took a lighter turn.

'Here you are, beginning to speak English fluently, but you've got an American accent. I suppose now you'd better try and learn the King's English!' said my father, laughing. 'It's just as well you studied that bit of French in Japan.'

It was our last serious talk together.

On 1 June, I said goodbye to Washington and my adolescence. We were given a big send-off as we boarded the train for San Francisco to embark on the *Shunyo Maru* for Japan, where the beginning of a new life awaited me.

I realize now how thoughtful it was the way my parents planned that sea voyage. They knew those two weeks would be my last carefree days so they saw to it that I thoroughly enjoyed myself, without thinking about the future. Nothing was said about my forth-coming life at court, for I am sure my father felt that to do so would only be counter-productive and plague me with anxieties and doubts.

I treasure a snapshot I have of my father lying in a deck-chair looking amused as he reads something on a small bit of paper. I had sat down beside him after a strenuous game of deck golf or quoits, and the the two of us look relaxed and happy. My parents left me quite free to play to my heart's content. I mostly played deck games alone, except for table-tennis, for which I had found a congenial companion.

I would have liked that happy voyage to go on forever, but the two weeks were over in a flash. On the other hand, it was nice to be coming home again after having been away for three years, and nostalgic thoughts crowded my mind as we dropped anchor off Yokohama early in the morning on 22 June.

In spite of it being June, there had been a storm the previous night, and the air was chilly. I put on a white coat over my blue dress, and completing the ensemble with a white hat, I went up on deck, where I could see a launch speeding towards us. Among the people at the bow I saw the smiling faces of my uncle and Count Kabayama. Soon, they were on board, accompanied by the Vice-Minister of the Imperial Household and other dignitaries, all of whom had come specially to greet me – who only yesterday had been playing on deck with complete abandonment! It brought home to me with a start that I was now on the way to belonging to another world.

A champagne toast was drunk in the lounge, and when the *Shunyo Maru* finally tied up at Pier No. 4, I was in for another surprise. I looked down from the deck to find the pier crowded with people. Surely they could not be there on my account, I thought, but the masses of schoolgirls standing in the rain, cheering and waving little rising sun flags were, in fact, to my great amazement, all there to welcome me. I waved back.

I followed my father down the gangway, led by the captain, in a blaze of newspaper flashbulbs and banks of newsreel cameras, to vociferous cheers of '*Banzai!*' I walked through it all in a daze, smiling and waving my handkerchief, to a room that had been prepared for us, where welcome speeches were made, and where I was reunited with Taka. Security was so strict that my brother Ichiro was unable to get in. Apparently the guards had refused to believe that he was Ambassador Matsudaira's eldest son.

We travelled to Tokyo in a special train, where another tremendous welcome awaited me. Among the crowd of well-wishers at the station I was particularly moved to find members of the former Aizu clan as well as five hundred girls, lined up in rows, representing all the girls schools in Tokyo.

I got in an automobile, my arms filled with bunches of flowers, and as we proceeded to our new house in the Shōto district of Shibuya Ward in a motorcade of ten cars, I knew there could be no turning back. I had already started out on the irrevocable path to a royal life. And no matter how difficult or strange it might be, I would not flinch. I vowed to do as my father had said and strive with all my heart to do my very best.

I have to admit that in spite of all my earlier determination and vows, at times I had been petrified and full of misgivings. But the fact that I had now seen for myself how delighted the people of Aizu were, and so many ordinary citizens, too, and how they all wished me happiness, was a great source of strength to me.

LEARNING TO BE A PRINCESS

The very day I returned home I received a message from the Empress Dowager to say I must be tired from the journey and would probably need to rest the following day, but that she would like me and my mother to come to her palace the day after that.

It was three years since Her Majesty had received us in audience. She graciously offered to teach me everything about court observances and etiquette, and asked me to come to her palace every day. Since there was no course of royal bridal instruction, with special teachers, as there is now, it was indeed reassuring for a completely unqualified ignoramus like me to know that I would be instructed personally by the Empress Dowager herself.

I had heard that the Empress Dowager, when she became the wife of the then Crown Prince, had herself received a rigorous training from those ladies-in-waiting who had served at court for a long time. The first thing I learned was how to walk. A good posture is essential for a princess. Long silk dresses, either low-necked or high-necked – referred to as *robes décolletées* and *robes montantes* – were worn at court functions, and it was considered indecorous to let one's shoes show when walking. One had to move gracefully, with elegance. And one had to learn how to put on ancient ceremonial robes and how to deport oneself in them. And when required to stand in attendance, one had to remain absolutely motionless for no matter how long.

My aunt Itsuko, Princess Nashimoto, did not marry her Prince until three years after their betrothal, since he was with his regiment in Hiroshima during that time. My cousin Masako, Princess Li – who was royal from birth – had a two-year wait. In my case I had barely three months. I could hardly be expected to learn everything in so short a time. I visited Her Majesty for instruction as frequently as possible and tried to remember everything she said, but it was all very difficult, and many were the times I shed tears in private.

Furthermore, only two months after our marriage, I would be required, as the consort of the Heir Presumptive, to attend upon the new Emperor and Empress at their enthronement in Kyoto.

Aunt Itsuko helped me a great deal, and said not to worry about the ceremonies – that I was sure to be instructed in the details at the time. She gave me much encouragement, urging me to relax and take things as they came. The words of cheerful, serene Aunt Itsuko always made my fears melt away like snow in springtime.

Writing poetry is a required accomplishment at the Imperial court, so I was given lessons in composing the traditional thirty-one syllable *waka* by Dr Taneaki Chiba, who had edited Emperor Meiji's poems for publication. I had calligraphy lessons from Dr Masaomi Ban.

On 12 July my parents, my uncle and aunt and I were invited to dinner by the Empress Dowager. Others invited were the Lord Keeper of the Privy Seal, the Minister and Vice-Minister for the Imperial Household, and other dignitaries. At this dinner I met Prince Chichibu for the first time since returning to Japan. A week later, on the 20th, His Imperial Highness hosted a dinner, to which I was invited, together with my parents, my elder brother, my sister, and my aunt and uncle. He invited my parents and me to dinner again on 29 August, and on 8 September; shortly after, we Matsudairas reciprocated with a dinner for the Prince.

I had now met His Highness four times before the ceremonial exchange of betrothal gifts took place on 14 September. For this occasion, my parents and I went to Uncle Morio's house, since I was now officially a member of his family. There, my uncle and aunt and I received the Prince's envoy. For this ceremony I wore a low-necked formal dress of snow-white silk and a necklace the Empress Dowager had given me.

The gold braid on the equerry's full-dress uniform sparkled as he relayed a message from His Imperial Highness, Yasuhito, Prince Chichibu, and a subordinate official gave orders for the betrothal gifts to be brought in. They consisted of an *uchiki* (a loose-fitting lined court robe of ancient design), a *hitoe* (an unlined summer court robe), a cedar-wood fan, sheets of special paper, a box containing a fresh sea-bream, and a barrel of *sake*, each presented on a plain wood stand.

When the envoy had left, our old retainers, who had come up to Tokyo the week before specially for this event, rejoiced together, with tears in their eyes.

Next day, the fifteenth, at ten in the morning, there was a ceremonial trying-on of the ancient-style court costume, called *junihitoe* (twelve unlined robes), that I was to wear at the wedding. The number of layers had fortunately been somewhat modified.

First, I had my hair done in the traditional way, stiffened with thick camellia oil and puffed well out at the sides into a sort of heart shape, with the rest tied in a pony-tail and hanging down at the back, greatly lengthened by the addition of a switch. The hairdresser began by combing the solid, lard-like pomade through my hair with a fine-tooth comb, which, as I remember, was very painful – much more so than with an ordinary old-fashioned Japanese hairdo – and needed great skill on the part of the hairdresser.

Even more skill was required on the part of the dresser. My dresser, seventy-year-old Seichoku Aoyama, had been with the Empress Dowager since her marriage. First, over a royal purple *kosode* (a short-sleeved under-kimono of soft silk), I put on a royal purple court *naga-bakama* (a full pleated divided skirt). It was so long that it seemed to be made for a giant, my feet coming where the giant's knees would be, and the rest trailing a long way behind. How would I ever walk in this without tripping! Next came the *hitoe*, a linen robe – unlined because it was summer – also in royal purple, followed by the *itsutsuginu*, or 'five robes', of deep royal crimson silk damask. Once they were five separate garments, but now just one, simulating five, with folds of shaded colours at the neck, the openings of the sleeves, and the edges of the skirt. Over all this went a lustrous purple linen *uchiginu* with wide sleeves, a pale blue double-woven outer robe (*uwagi*) lined with yellow silk, and finally a *karaginu*, or 'Chinese jacket' of blue brocade. A trailing, pleated fan-shaped train was attached at the back from my waist. Combs, hair ornaments, a cedar-wood fan and a brocade paper-case completed my outfit.

I learned of the importance of neatly lining up the collars of the first three robes, and that it was essential that the hems of the garments as they trailed out to either side from the sash, being longer than one's height also be neatly aligned. The dresser and assistants arranged the robes while I merely stood there like a mannequin. Although the garments were 'summer weight', some were lined, making the costume heavy, and the many layers made it hard to move my arms. I wondered how I would get through the ceremony. I quailed at the thought of the 'winter weight' set I would be wearing for the ceremonies connected with the November enthronement.

My mother was obviously relieved that her sister, Princess Itsuko, was on hand to advise and guide me. As the wedding day drew near, she relayed to me a message from my aunt that I should drink very little tea and other liquids from the day before the ceremony.

I noticed that mother spoke to me employing verbal forms used when addressing a superior. She had started doing this the day of the Exchange of Betrothal Gifts. Although I knew that our old mother-daughter relationship was bound to undergo this change, I could not help but feel sad. 'You must not think of Setsuko as a Matsudaira any more', she had told my sister and brothers. 'And you must change your way of speaking to her.'

THE LAST FEW DAYS

Before the betrothal ceremony, on 26 July 1928, I toured our old family fief of Aizu – now Fukushima Prefecture – for four days with my aunt and uncle, my parents, my elder brother, my sister, and Taka. I went to report my forthcoming marriage at the graves of my ancestors and to bid farewell to our former clansmen, who shed tears of joy, exclaiming that the honour of Aizu had been restored.

I had only been once before to Aizu, and that was to the spa at Yanaizu on the Tadami river, and it was my parents who had been wined and dined and made a fuss of then. This time it was I who was the VIP – already royal in their eyes. 'Princess Setsuko comes to Aizu' proclaimed a local newspaper headline.

I was getting used to being addressed as Princess, but I found crowd ovations unnerving. It was not until I listened to the solemn declaration made by my uncle Morio at Hanitsu Shrine – dedicated to the memory of Lord Hoshina, founder of our clan – that I fully understood the import of what was expected of me:

'I hereby inform the spirits of my ancestors' he intoned, 'that Morio Matsudaira's niece and Tsuneo Matsudaira's daughter Setsuko is to be married to His Imperial Highness Prince Chichibu. I hereby vow that she will endeavour to bcome a paragon of Japanese womanhood.'

As we visited various parts of the province, I was given a tremendous welcome by four hundred thousand former vassals. The knowledge that the people of Aizu were so overjoyed about my marrying into the Imperial Family made me determine anew to strive my utmost, no matter how difficult it might be, to live up to the Empress Dowager's expectations.

On 17 September, the spelling of my name was changed, because the Empress Dowager's name, though pronounced Sadako, was written with the same first Chinese character as mine – namely that meaning 'season'. From several alternative characters suggested by the Empress Dowager's chief chamberlain, Mr Irie, Her Majesty chose the character for 'se' as in Ise, the site of the Great Shinto Shrine, and the character for 'tsu' (also pronounced 'zu') as in my ancestral Aizu.

On the twentieth, my trousseau was sent from our house to Prince Chichibu's palace in Akasaka. There were various chests, and chests of drawers – some lacquered black, others plain wood – as well as personal effects, clothes and other paraphernalia. The same day, accompanied by my mother, I called upon the Emperor and Empress, the Empress Dowager, and all the princes and princesses to pay my final respects as Setsuko Matsudaira.

The following days were full, with farewell parties being given for me almost every day by former schoolmates, friends, teachers and associates, which fortunately left me little time to brood on my forthcoming marriage. One whole room in our house was filled with wedding presents, including gifts from the President of the United States and the Secretary of State.

The lingering summer heat was finally over by 26 September, and there was a slight drizzle when the Ceremony of the Announcement took place at Uncle Morio's house, at which Prince Chichibu formally made known to the Matsudaira family the date set for the marriage. From early that morning the principal members of the former Aizu clan began converging on the house, and in due course the Prince's envoy arrived. My uncle, in his rear-admiral's dress uniform, my father in tails, and my mother and aunt in formal kimono, waited in a row in the upstairs drawing-room, while I stood in my appointed place in a pink frock. As soon as he had been led in by the butler, the envoy – the Prince's private secretary – solemnly announced: 'I hereby inform Setsuko Matsudaira that the marriage ceremony will take place on 28 September in the third year of Shōwa', to which my uncle replied, on my behalf: 'With humble duty, she will be pleased to comply.' It was all over in half an hour.

'What a moment of emotion,' wrote Taka in her diary. 'A half-year's agonizing gone like ice in the spring sun.'

That evening, we gave a dinner at home for me to say farewell to my close friends as well as those who had served the family for many years. Taka's diary describes it better than I could:

'We, too, were invited,' she wrote, 'the butler, the houseboys, the maids, and I, on the same equal footing as the distinguished guests. "There's to be no formality," His Lordship told us warmly. There was a feel of autumn in the air as we sat down to dinner a little after six. You could not blame those members of the Aizu clan for their joy after years of grieving over the fall of the Castle. I, who had never danced in my life, was so overcome with emotion that I found myself joining in the folkdance with tears in my eyes, although I did not know the steps. How Lady Setsuko must have smiled to herself when she saw me. To think this was Lady Setsuko's last night in this house! To think this was her farewell to those of us gathered there. During a pause in the dancing, she stood up, looking like a flower, and thanked us all in a clear voice, and the guests started dancing again around her like a garland of flowers.

'She had gifts for us all. Mine was a wristwatch she had bought in Washington. She handed it to me saying: "You've been so good to me for seventeen years. Take care of yourself, won't you." Then she said, "I've got something else for you," and went to her room and brought me a little box with three drawers, which she said I was not to open until afterwards. It reminded me of the fairytale and the treasure casket the princess gave the young fisherman, Urashima Taro, when he left the Dragon Palace under the sea. Tears welled up in my eyes, as I wondered what was inside. "You've been crying ever since this morning," she chided me, but I could see something glistening in her bright eyes too. "Just today," I replied. "Please allow me to cry a little, just today."'

Late that night – the last night I would sleep in my old home – I expressed to my mother and father, in just a few words, my heartfelt gratitude for all they had done for me, and the way they had brought me up these past twenty years. It was my way of saying goodbye. As for daddy, all he said was: 'I can only repeat what I've always said you must do: put your heart and soul into doing your very best.'

Mother said: 'I am praying for your happiness. Be sure and take good care of your health.'

Their eyes overflowed with love and affection and the myriad thoughts that filled their minds. We did not give way to tears.

> *May integrity*
> *Be my strength, as like a ship*
> *On a stormy sea,*
> *I ride out the wild billows*
> *Of this world's deceit and lies.*

My father liked this *waka* and used to inscribe it in his graceful calligraphy. I remembered the poem, and it gave me courage as I thought of the bumpy road ahead that I must do my utmost to negotiate well.

# CHAPTER FIVE

# *Imperial Bride*

## THE TWELVE-LAYERED ROBE

O n 27 September, the day before my wedding, I ate my last lunch as a member of the Matsudaira family, and after going with my mother to the Empress Dowager's palace to pay our respects, we set off from home, bound for my uncle Morio's house, at about four in the afternoon – my parents, brothers and sister, Taka and I. A crowd of neighbours were gathered outside the gate to see me off, including children from the nearby primary school waving little Rising Sun flags.

As soon as we arrived, Taka helped me change into kimono for a farewell family dinner to which our domestic staff had also been invited. Not wanting it to be a sad occasion, Aunt Tomoko said cheerfully, 'Setsuko, you may not have much opportunity to eat tomorrow, so you must eat as much as you can tonight and get plenty of nourishment.' Everyone laughed. Aunt Tomoko was the widow of my uncle Katamori, the late Lord Matsudaira, and was the oldest there. Although I was under a certain amount of strain, knowing it was my last family dinner, it was a jolly and enjoyable evening.

Mother, Taka and I spent the night at Uncle Morio's. As soon as the others had gone, I had my bath after which the Imperial hairdresser washed my hair and completed its preliminary pomading. The moon, which was almost full, had just risen, and I entered my bedroom to find it flooded with brightness. I opened the window. If only mother and I could enjoy the view for a few last intimate moments together, I thought. But it was not to be. Reminding me that I must make a very early start the following morning, she insisted that I go straight to bed.

I had to rise just after two – long before daybreak. I breakfasted between the various stages of being made up, having my hair done, and being dressed in the so-called 'twelve-layered robe'. The great weight of the combined garments seemed to me to symbolize the weight of the duties I was taking upon myself in becoming a member of the Imperial Family.

I left the house at 8.15 – exactly the same time, as I learned later, that His Highness, Yasuhito, had left his palace. The whole Matsudaira family were gathered under the *porte cochère* of my uncle's mansion, where a maroon state carriage drawn by two horses awaited me. A lady-in-waiting, Mrs Yamaza, dressed in white, took my hand and helped me into the carriage, neatly arranging the trailing trouser-legs of my divided skirt, and sat opposite me. I must have been nervous and apprehensive as we started off, for I scarcely took heed of the servants and Taka, who stood dabbing their eyes with handkerchiefs.

My uncle's residence stood in a rather hilly area and

apparently there had been some question as to whether the carriage could safely negotiate the slopes, but the journey went off without hitch and lady-in-waiting Yamaza was a most considerate companion. The roads were lined with people, and I can still see them in my mind's eye, waving their little Rising Sun flags.

When we arrived at the entrance to the *Kashiko-dokoro* – the sanctuary inside the Palace grounds – the lady-in-waiting helped me out of the carriage, and I bowed low to the waiting Prince, who bowed in return.

In a dressing-room, the traditional three-pronged gold coronet-like ornament was placed in my hair, and in my hands was placed the ceremonial cedar-wood fan symbolizing feminine modesty.

At precisely nine o'clock, to the strains of the *shichiriki* and *shō* – the flutes and mouth-organs of the thousand-year-old court orchestra – the Chief Ritualist in traditional robes made an offering to the gods and intoned a prayer. Then, led by another ritualist, His Highness proceeded along the gallery, holding a sceptre, followed by me, and we entered the outer chamber of the sanctuary. Although nowadays much of these ceremonies is televised, cameras are still not allowed inside the sanctuary, and since my recollection of the actual marriage service has become dim, I shall quote from an account by one of the ritualists.

'His Highness sat on the right facing the altar, and Her Highness on the left. First, His Highness bowed to both sanctums (Her Highness doing likewise) and then reported earnestly and in a clear voice: "At this auspicious time on this auspicious day, we conduct this ceremony of marriage before Thee. We solemnly vow that henceforth and forevermore we shall live together in mutual love and fellowship that shall not change for one thousand, nay, ten thousand generations." Then a ritualist set a small wooden stand with an earthenware cup on it before each of Their Highnesses and Chief Ritualist Kujo took the vessel of sacred *sake* and poured it for them. At exactly eight minutes past nine, the loud boom of a cannon rent the silence of the autumn air above the Palace, followed by another and another as the twenty-one gun salute continued and Their Highnesses quietly left the palace looking as beautiful and elegant as figures in the Hina Festival. What a splendid and congenial pair they made!'

Guests had been invited to observe the procession to and from the Sanctuary. They included all members of the nobility, the Minister for the Imperial Household, and other high government officials. My uncle Morio and my aunt, as well as my parents, were special guests. I wondered what they thought when they heard the gun salute and watched me leave the Sanctuary as a princess.

Yasuhito, Prince Chichibu, born in June, 1902, was twenty-six, and I had just turned nineteen.

'PINETREES TWAIN'

A state coach was drawn up outside the Sanctuary, and I followed the Prince into it and sat by his side. Led by a cavalcade bearing the Imperial standard, we crossed Nijū Bridge and left the Palace grounds, where we were joined by a mounted guard of honour in white-plumed helmets, carrying standards, and proceeded in ceremonial order to the Prince's residence in Akasaka. Both sides of the road were thronged with people holding little Rising Sun flags, and I could hear their cheers of '*Banzai! Banzai!*' as I sat rigidly facing straight ahead, trying not to lose my balance as the carriage swayed.

In those days, people had to bow respectfully when royalty passed by, and were not allowed to look at them. It was not like it is now when people can freely look at us and wave their flags, and we can wave back and smile.

When we arrived at the *porte cochère* of the Prince's residence, the guard of honour lined up as the Prince's private secretary, Mr. Maeda, opened the door of our carriage and the lady-in-waiting took my hand and helped me out. I stood with my head bowed as the Prince alighted, and stood beside him to bow our respects to his four aunts, who had arrived ahead of us – Nobuko, Princess Asaka; Toshiko, Princess Higashi-kuni; Fusako, Princess Kitashirakawa; and Masako, Princess Takeda; – the daughters of Emperor Meiji. I remember being very nervous, as these were the elder princesses whose guidance I would be seeking, and whose admonitions I would have to heed.

The ceremony of the 'three-times-three' exchange of nuptial *sake* cups was performed anew, after which we sat down to a banquet – I still in my 'twelve-layered' robe and the Prince in his ancient court costume. A friend who was a young lady-in-waiting at the time tells me how graceful I looked as I poured the *sake* for His Highness, but I felt far from graceful, and I imagine it was the beauty of the ancient Heian Period garb that fascinated her. Neither she nor I can remember who poured the *sake* for me. It was probably Lady-in-waiting Yamaza. Neither can I remember what exactly we were served at the ceremonial banquet – only how varied and colourful the many dishes were.

After the meal, we had our photographs taken and then, in what was to be my upstairs living-quarters,

Lady-in-waiting Yamaza and a maid had hurriedly to help me out of the many robes, wash the stiffening out of my hair, and dress and coif me anew for the ceremonial audience with the Emperor and Empress.

Removing the hair grease was a dreadful ordeal. My hair first had to be wiped with benzine and then given a good scrubbing, and even though they bound a cloth tightly around my eyes, the fabric inevitably became wet, and the soap, mixed with fumes from the benzine, got into my eyes. They stung excruciatingly, but worse than that, I was temporarily blinded. It was frightening. I wondered if my sight would ever return. The relief was enormous as the pain and the blackness gradually receded.

With feverish haste, my hair was arranged anew, and I was dressed in the formal European court gown provided for me by the Empress Dowager. It had a long train, which I would carry over my left arm. When worn at the New Year's Day ceremony it would be held by two young boys of the nobility.

The sash of the Order of the Sacred Crown, First Class, worn by consorts of Imperial princes, was fixed across my bosom diagonally down from the right shoulder, and the heavy diamond-encrusted badge was fastened nearby. A sparkling diamond tiara and gold brocaded pumps completed the outfit.

The Prince changed, too, into the ceremonial dress uniform of an infantry lieutenant, and held his plumed hat while we had our photographs taken. Meanwhile, the Prince's secretary kept coming in, at ten minute intervals, to inform us of the arrival of wedding gifts – a sword, a clock, and a magnificent sea-bream – symbol of good fortune – from the Emperor, a brooch from the Empress, and another bream from the Empress Dowager.

We then took our places once more in the state coach to ride back to the Imperial Palace. The crowds lining the road were still there, and greeted us with undiminished fervour. This time I felt a little more relaxed, and in my heart I kept saying: 'Thank you, everybody!'

We crossed the moat again by the graceful bridge called 'Nijū-bashi' and alighting at the Western Chamber, we made our way into the Phoenix Room, I dragging my heavy train. This was an important ceremonial occasion in which we formally announced our marriage to Their Majesties.

As soon as the Emperor and Empress had taken their places on the dais, the Grand Chamberlain led us to our places below, and after the Prince had expressed his gratitude to the Emperor, His Majesty conveyed his felicitations to us in ancient court language, and so did the Empress. Then, the Prince and I sat down in the seats that had been provided for us, and a chamberlain and a lady-in-waiting brought us each a tray with *sake* and food and poured *sake* for Their Majesties. It was a special thick, black *sake* called *kunen-shu*, or 'nine-year *sake*', made by boiling black soybeans, *sake* and *mirin* (sweet *sake*). Before Their Majesties had partaken thereof, the chamberlain first handed the Emperor's cup to the Prince, then the lady-in-waiting handed the Empress's cup to me, and we partook. After that we took up our chopsticks and made as if to begin eating, but did not in fact do so, since it was only a symbolic gesture. This ended the ceremony, and the Prince and I rose and bowed deeply as Their Majesties departed.

We continued in our carriage to the Eastern Palace in Aoyama to pay our respects to the Empress Dowager, who received us warmly, and gazing with great affection, first at the Prince and then at me by his side who was now his wife, she spoke the ancient words of felicitation, but the message she conveyed with her eyes as she spoke was a fervent hope that we would be happy together in love and comradeship. And she composed the following poem:

> *So many people*
>   *Wish you great happiness,*
>     *With all their heart.*
> *Let their joy not be in vain,*
> *O pinetrees twain!*

The autumn dusk was falling by the time we arrived back at our residence. The lamp at the gate was already lit, and glows faintly still in my memory, like a daytime moon.

There was no relaxing yet, however. I had to be helped out of my court gown and into a formal black kimono patterned with cranes and ocean waves woven with gold and silver threads.

Since the day before, I had been dressed by others, just as if I were a doll or mannequin. It seemed appropriate then, as the garments were all so unfamiliar, but now it was different. I bent down quite naturally, without thinking, to fasten the clasps of my *tabi*, the white silk foot mittens one wears with kimono.

'No, no!' cried my elderly lady-in-waiting emphatically, 'You must let me do that.' I was taken aback. Was I to remain a mannequin forever, I wondered in dismay. My sister had been a delicate child and Taka had spent more time looking after her than me, so from the time I was quite small I had learned to do everything for myself. The idea of allowing someone else to fasten my footwear seemed preposterous.

But I had no time for thoughts such as this. Whilst my costume was busily being changed, a messenger came to say that Prince Sumi had arrived to see us. The sweet playful youth I had last seen at the Nikko Imperial villa was already a pupil at a military preparatory school. I went downstairs to find that Prince Chichibu had also just come down – now dressed in a formal black crested kimono jacket and *hakama* trousers – and together we received the congratulations of his young brother, who cut an imposing figure in his uniform.

The night was brilliant with the light of the full moon. Led by bands, groups of marchers had been coming by since early evening – local residents of Akasaka, five thousand boy scouts, groups five thousand strong made up of each of the other Tokyo wards – and finally five thousand people carrying paper lanterns. Representatives from each group had come in through the side gate and were lined up opposite the *porte-cochère*. They probably only intended to express their felicitations to a footman or secretary and retire, but when the Prince heard they were there, he jumped up, motioning me to follow, and hurried outside – in his indoor slippers! I did not take the time to change into outdoor footwear either. In fact it all happened so quickly there was no time, anyway, for anyone to have got them out.

The Prince, with spontaneous ease, thanked the representatives most warmly, while I bowed beside him. In those days, to be spoken to personally by a member of the Imperial Family was so unbelievable and awe-inspiring that the representatives were rendered speechless with emotion. Some time after we had returned inside and the people had gone, we heard thunderous shouts of '*banzai!*' coming in waves from the crowds. Perhaps those representatives had passed the word to those outside of their unexpected encounter.

That night, I was told, people from far and wide had gathered in Hibiya Park, thrilled to see a newsreel of the wedding, although it merely consisted of a few minutes of the procession, sandwiched among sports items. What a far cry from television coverage today!

The hum of voices from the lantern parade had receded into the distance like the sound of far-off surf when the Ceremony of the Rice Cakes – symbolizing the conjugal tie – took place in our bedroom, conducted by lady-in-waiting Yamaza and private secretary Maeda. Inside a box made of beautiful, heavy handmade paper, were two earthenware bowls, each piled high with twenty tiny white rice cakes the size of *go* counters – twenty because that was my age. After the Prince and I made symbolic gestures as if to eat the rice cakes, the box was left in the room, and after three days it was buried in the garden in a spot deemed propitious.

The fateful day in which I took my first steps as a princess, 28 September 1928, finally drew to its close. It had been a long day, with one new experience following another in quick succession. 'You must be terribly tired. It'll all take a lot of getting used to, I know. But don't worry – I'll always be there for you to lean on.'

The Prince's voice was warm and caring, but I was too stiff and awkward even to raise my face to his.

'I know so little. I wish to learn from you, my lord.'

I think I said something like that, and I faintly remember making a deep bow.

THE CHRYSANTHEMUM AND I

As soon as I awoke on my first morning as a princess, Lady-in-waiting Yamaza, who was on duty in the next room, came in, with a respectful bow, to help me wash and dress. I greeted her with special warmth, for not only was I grateful for her devoted help the day before, but I had discovered who she was. By one of those curious coincidences, Shizuka Yamaza turned out to be the widow of Enjiro Yamaza – *chargé d'affaires* at the Japanese Embassy in London when I was born – who had been asked by my father to select a name for me. It is a Japanese custom to ask some respected person to do this. I did not learn of this connection until just before the wedding, when I had little time to think about it. There could be no familiarity between us, of course, for court protocol dictated that Mrs. Yamaza and I must treat each other as mistress and servant, but as she waited upon me I sensed a touching solicitude, and although we could not express it in words, we both were aware of a deep understanding between us.

The *chargé d'affaires* in London, my father's boss, had suggested two names: Setsu (season) or Kiku (chrysanthemum), since I was born on the ninth day of the ninth month – the Chrysanthemum Festival of ancient observance. My father chose Setsu, and my mother then took the chrysanthemum for my emblem. (It used to be the custom for members of royalty and the aristocracy in Japan to have their own sign, or emblem, with which to mark their clothes and other possessions.) When my mother, the daughter of Marquis Nabeshima, chose this flower as her daughter's mark, little did she know that her child would one day ascend the precincts of the Chrysanthemum Throne. It was strange how fate was to bind us – the Yamazas, the Chrysanthemum, and I.

The Prince's emblem was a young pine.

The first visit we made together on the day after our marriage was to the Emperor and Empress to express our thanks. The Empress spoke to me most kindly, which was very heartening. After that we called upon the Empress Dowager, who seemed particularly delighted to see us and said we must come often, urging me to come in kimono.

Nowadays, it is permitted to wear kimono openly at court, but before the war the official dress was Western-style. Kimono could only be worn, after dark, at private family gatherings, and one had to enter the palace by a side door, passing through the gardens. I therefore had very few kimonos in my dowry, but I used to try and wear a different one each time we called upon Her Majesty.

Having only sons, I believe she enjoyed seeing me in my colourful kimonos, and I think the Prince did too. Many was the time she would not let us go until after eleven.

The second week after the wedding our household was kept busy with celebratory dinners, teas and audiences, as well as state visits to the Ise Shrine and the Imperial mausolea. In addition, my personal effects and clothes had to be carefully organized and sorted out. The people of Aizu shed tears of joy when they learned that the court had given permission for me to use the Matsudaira hollyhock crest on my things, and that on the day of the marriage I had with me the fine family heirloom sword by Kunitoshi Rai, in its brocade bag.

I was not allowed to help sort and put away any of my belongings, except for making a few suggestions. Merely touching an ornamental bird in the garden to adjust its position brought a cry of, 'I will do that Ma'am!' I should have known better by then, having been prevented even from fastening my own *tabi*, but on my first evening visit to the Empress Dowager in kimono I thoughtlessly started to turn my footwear around at the entrance after slipping them off, but was hurriedly prevented from doing so. I would have preferred to carry out this point of Japanese etiquette myself, for I knew how I liked to place them for easy slipping into on departure. Moreover, I was amazed to note that services to do with the lower part of the body and those to do with the upper part were rendered by different attendants. Oh dear, I thought, and wondered what other surprises were in store for me. How I wished Taka were there. I thought of the little box with three drawers that I had given her the night of the farewell dinner, telling her not to open it until later, and pictured her laughing and perhaps shedding a few tears at what was inside. I cannot remember exactly what they were, but they were the things I treasured as a child. I was leaving my childhood in her safekeeping as I set out to do my best as a princess, and I am quite sure she understood.

My aunt, Princess Itsuko, had said: 'Patience and perseverance are the most important attributes. If you have these, you will soon learn to be a princess.' I realized I would have to forget the ways I was used to, and learn to do things the court way as fast as I could. It would indeed require patience and perseverance.

October was soon upon us and a string of formal functions began on the fourth. On the third, the Prince went alone to Yokohama to welcome back his brother Midshipman Prince Nobuhito Takamatsu who was returning from a cruise that had prevented him attending our wedding.

On the fourth, there was a banquet at the Akasaka Palace attended by the Imperial Family, ambassadors and ministers from twenty-five countries, and their wives, Grand Master of Ceremonies Hirokuni Ito, Lord

Keeper of the Privy Seal Count Makino, and various Foreign Ministry officials including my father, the ambassador designate to Great Britain. It was my first experience of such an international gathering.

On the fifth, we received the congratulations of three hundred members of the various embassies and the Imperial Household staff at a reception at the Akasaka Palace.

On the sixth, we hosted a purely family banquet at which the Prince's maternal family was represented by Prince Kujō and mine by Viscount Matsudaira – my uncle Morio. His daughters – my cousins – were invited too, and were entertained with lively conversation by Prince Takamatsu, sun-tanned from his recent overseas voyage.

One day I gave a party for the ladies-in-waiting, and on another day we held a reception at the Akasaka Palace for over two hundred people who included our former teachers, close friends and classmates, as well as the Prince's sports associates.

And then on the eleventh, there was a banquet at the Akasaka Palace for the Imperial Family and senior members of each princely house, as well as the Prime Minister and top brass. Finally, on the twelfth, there was a luncheon for almost two hundred military and government personnel, among which the Prince was especially happy to honour Colonel Nagata, the commanding officer of the Third Infantry Regiment, of which the Prince was an officer.

There had been a reception that same day for over six hundred of the men of the regiment – so many there was hardly enough room for them all in the Akasaka Palace. I was deeply impressed at the way the Prince meticulously observed respect for the senior officers with no sign of the fact that he was heir to the throne, and by the easy camaraderie he showed to his fellow officers. It was a side of him that I had not seen before.

While all the official receptions and banquets were now over, leaving me quite depleted both mentally and physically, so new and unfamiliar had everything been to me, the days that followed were still full of engagements.

On the thirteenth we attended an international swimming meet in honour of our marriage at Tokyo's only fifty-metre pool, which was in Tamagawa. The contestants were all swimmers who had taken part in the Amsterdam Olympics, and afterwards the Prince chatted with many of them, including America's Johnny Weismuller of Tarzan fame.

The following evening we dined at the home of Mr Devison, the British Consul, to meet the visiting wife of retired Major-General Laurence Drummond. The Drummonds had provided a home away from home for the Prince throughout his year of study in Britain, so the reunion was a nostalgic one for him. The Prince had a special affection for Britain, and had been Patron of the Japan-British Society since that January. He wanted the Empress Dowager to meet Mrs Drummond, so we arranged a tea in our garden the following day to which we also invited the British Ambassador, Sir John Tilley, and Lady Tilley.

Not only was I a very new member of the Imperial Family, but I was a totally inexperienced hostess, and having to entertain foreigners made me very nervous indeed. But the Empress Dowager, the Ambassador and his wife and Mrs Drummond were so congenial that I felt a great sense of relief.

Needless to say, I could never have coped with all these unfamiliar duties that had been thrust upon my

shoulders had it not been for the support and help of
the staff. But above all, it was the moral support given
me by the Prince that kept me going from day to day.
He was my source of spiritual strength with his
encouragement and his caring consideration. Three
days after our wedding, when there was still so much
to learn and I seemed to be confounded whichever
way I turned, the Prince was obviously concerned for
me in my predicament and did his best to reassure me.

'I know how it must be,' he said, with sympathy and
understanding. 'There's far more than I could teach
you. It's best if you just take things as they come. Don't
worry! You'll absorb it all naturally, bit by bit.'

From that day on, I knew I could rely on the Prince
to be my tower of strength, and that everything would
be all right if I did as he said. I also knew that I would
do anything in the world for him, and that nothing
would be too hard.

All the Tokyo ceremonies in connection with our
marriage were now over. It only remained to pay our
respects at the Grand Shrine at Ise and the Imperial
tombs. We set off on a special train westbound for the
area around Kyoto and Nara – the ancient capitals of
Japan – and within the month had made our obeisances
at Ise, at the mausoleum of Emperor Jimmu – the first
Japanese emperor – which stands at the foot of Mount
Unebi, and at the tombs of the Prince's grandfather,
Emperor Meiji, and his father, Emperor Taishō.

CHAPTER SIX

# *The Silver Drum*

A BROTHERLY CHAT

*E*ven though the functions connected with our
marriage were over, there was no time to start
living the life of normal newly-weds for preparations
had to be made to depart for the Enthronement on 6
November in Kyoto where we would attend on Their
Majesties. I would have to lead all the other princesses
during the ancient ceremonies, and I was sure I would
find myself completely at sea. I would just have to do
the best I could. I did my utmost to learn what I had to
do. I am sure the Empress Dowager and the Prince
were as worried as I was about my performance. I was
instructed in the rules of etiquette by the ritualists, but
would I remember what do do when the time actually
came to do it?

On the sixth of November we left Tokyo as part of
the Imperial *cortège*, spending the night at the
Tokugawa mansion in Nagoya. The following day, we
continued the journey to Kyoto, where we spent the

night at the Sumitomo mansion in Shishigatani. On the tenth, the first two enthronement ceremonies took place – one before the Sanctuary (the *Kashiko-dokoro*, which had been brought with us from Tokyo) and the other in the Shishinden, or State Ceremonial Hall. The following day there were ancient ceremonial shrine dances, and on the fourteenth, the *daijōsai* – the Emperor's mystical rite of all-night communion with his ancestors, which goes back to time immemorial.

Banquets were held on the sixteenth and seventeenth, and after that we accompanied Their Majesties to the Grand Shrine at Ise and the Imperial Tombs.

With the Emperor and Empress and their Court all dressed in the ancient style, the age-old enthronement ceremonies must have seemed like a beautiful antique screen or scroll come to life. I remember, however, the enormous weight of my 'twelve-layered' robe – winter-weight, as opposed to the summer-weight robe I wore at my wedding. I heard later that it probably weighed between fifteen and sixteen kilograms!

I also remember the care we princesses had to exercise in regard to the Parisian gowns – both high neck and *decolletée* – worn at the state banquets and some of the ceremonies, to ensure that the colours we chose did not clash with that worn by the Empress or predominate over it. If Her Majesty was not present, it was the colour of my gown which took precedence, since I was the bride of the Heir Presumptive, and the ladies-in-waiting of the various princesses would enquire of mine as to what I intended to wear.

The same rule applied, whatever the occasion. I could not see the point of this at first, and wondered what was wrong with variety in dress, but that was the way it was and one had to abide by palace custom. For example, if we wore a fur, it would not only have to be

*Formal study of Prince and Princess Chichibu in 1936*

ABOVE *Princess Chichibu aged two with brother Ichiro.* RIGHT: *Dressed as a Red Cross nurse with friend at a flood relief bazaar in Tienstin, c.1916*

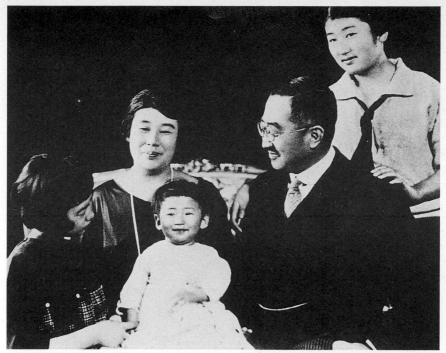

*Princess Chichibu, aged 15, standing (right) with her family at the Embassy residence, Washington, DC, 1924*

*Portrait taken at the time of her graduation from the Friends School, Washington, aged 18*

*Prince Chichibu in his academic gown, after receiving an honorary degree from Oxford University, 23 May 1937*

*Family 'farewell' garden party for Princess Chichibu (far right) prior to her marriage in 1928*

*With Prince Chichibu on the sea front at Hove, England, April 1937*

*Hiking with the Prince in the mountains of Nagano Prefecture*

*In conversation for a magazine profile*

*The Prince and Princess taking tea in their villa at Gotemba.*
*[Photo: FRANCIS HAAR]*

*A rare 'personal' photograph (c.1948-50) of Princess Chichibu*
*attending to her hair using hand mirrors decorated with the*
*Matsudaira family crest. [Photo: FRANCIS HAAR]*

*Photographed with Prime Minister Harold MacMillan at Admiralty House, London, 24 July 1962.*
[Photo: HULTON DEUTSCH]

*Princess Chichibu receiving Eleanor Roosevelt and American women journalists (the Princess's mother on Mrs Roosevelt's right) c.1956*

*Statue of Prince Chichibu in the gardens of the villa at Gotemba looking across to Mount Fuji*

*Princess Chichibu discusses roses with the late Lady Keswick's sister Lady Morland (wife of Sir Oscar Morland, Ambassador to Japan 1959-63) at the Keswick's home in Scotland in 1974*

*Princess Chichibu admiring a bonzai tree on a visit to the Royal Horticultural Society gardens at Wisley in 1979. [Photo: THE TIMES]*

the same kind as the others, but worn with the head of the animal facing exactly the same way. I simply could not understand why one could not wear one's stole any way one wished, and the sight of us all wearing identical silver-fox furs in an identical manner used to strike me as most odd.

I think it was the day before the Enthronement Ceremony that I came upon Prince Chichibu and the Emperor having a happy *tête-a-tête* in a dimly-lit room of the Palace in Kyoto. The brothers had not had the opportunity for a chat for some time, and they were talking and laughing in a relaxed, informal way about something that interested them both, although I do not recall what it was.

In those days, in accordance with the Meiji Constitution, the Emperor, since his succession, had become a divine sovereign up in the clouds. And so, as I watched these two, between whom there now existed such a clear line of demarcation talking together for a little while just like any ordinary brothers, I realized anew the awesome character of the realm into which I had married. I still remember the qualms that assailed me at that moment.

We accompanied Their Majesties back to Tokyo on the twenty-seventh and attended the *mikagura* shrine dances before the Palace Sanctuary on the following day. That evening, we hosted a dinner for the American Ambassador and Mrs McVeigh. I had not met them before, but after having lived and studied in their country for three years, they seemed like old and dear friends.

The days that followed were filled with official engagements – some for the Prince alone, some for us both. We attended a dinner at the British Embassy, and there were lunches and dinners at the palace for the foreign diplomatic corps, and I discovered how busy members of the Imperial Family were, with their schedules crammed with diplomatic engagements and public service duties.

On 20 December, my parents invited us to dinner. It was not only my first visit home since my marriage, but a farewell to my parents, who were to leave in a week's time for London, where my father had been appointed Ambassador. Outwardly, we were making a royal visit to the house of a loyal subject, so we were naturally attended by equerries and ladies-in-waiting, with a police escort, and my family were formally lined up at the entrance to receive us.

I felt strange and uncomfortable being received as royalty by my own kith and kin, and thought how curious it was that I had stood myself in a similar line at the door of the Japanese Embassy in Washington when the Prince had arrived there the year before.

The Prince chatted to everyone with friendly ease, and when my father showed him over the house, he nonchalantly sat on the railing of the upstairs veranda and gazed into the garden, giving my mother palpitations for fear the railing might give way. He wanted to see everything, including my room, which was still just as I had left it.

I was wearing kimono, and formerly Taka would have taken a lively interest in how I looked in it, but now she kept her eyes lowered the whole time and hardly said a word, which was like her, but still made me sad.

The Prince enjoyed talking to my father regarding his prospective London appointment and about his own time of study in England. My parents did their best to make it an enjoyable evening, and the Prince seemed to relish the family atmosphere, which was a pleasant change from the usual formal banquet.

Four days later the Prince entered the Military Academy. He had been ordered to do so by Imperial command. He had already been tutored in military history, strategy and tactics by Lieutenant-Colonel Honma, his aide, who had once been an instructor at the Academy, and who had been appointed aide-de-camp to the Prince just after the late Emperor's death. The colonel had spent three years in England studying military affairs and so the Prince found him most companionable.

On 26 December, my father left for England with his family to take up his appointment as Ambassador, again leaving behind my elder brother Ichiro, now a student at Mito High School, and taking with them Taka and her son Ryō.

A YOUNG PINE AND A STAR

So unused was I to my new life that at times I felt like a bird that had lost its way and flown into the wrong place, and I would be filled with despair at my incompetence.

'Don't let it worry you if you make a mistake', the Prince would say. 'Nobody can get used to a new life right away. You'll learn it all gradually.'

But I could hardly bother him with every little thing, so what used to provide me with constant comfort was the *bonbonnière* given to me by the Empress Dowager.

At the Japanese Court it is the custom to give small silver confection boxes – known by the French word *bonbonnière* – as mementos to mark special occasions. Much thought is given to their design, with the occasion in mind, so that each one is unique. The boxes contain those tiny old-fashioned sugar-drops that used to be known as comfits. It is a custom peculiar to the Japanese Court and aristocracy, and is reminiscent of the Fabergé easter-eggs once exchanged by Russian royalty.

The Empress Dowager gave me the *bonbonnière* at the dinner she gave for me upon my return from the United States. The Minister for the Imperial Household had been invited, and other dignitaries, and after the banquet, Her Majesty called the Prince and me over to her and handed the gifts to each of us personally. She had designed the silver memento herself. It was a miniature *tsuzumi*, the ancient Japanese hand drum shaped like an hourglass. Fine rose-coloured silk cord had been used for the tension-adjusting drum-rope, and the body of the drum was embossed with a pattern of tiny young pines and stars. The young pines were the Prince's symbol, the rose-coloured cord was for England, where he had studied, and the stars were for the Stars and Stripes of America where I had been to school. Her Majesty's hope that our union would bring England, America and Japan closer together was beautifully expressed in her touchingly thought-out gift.

Looking at this ancient musical instrument reproduced in miniature I cannot help feeling how modern it seems today. The rose-coloured cord has been replaced, but the silver is as bright as ever and I keep this treasured memento in a glass case in my drawing-room. I often pick it up and marvel anew at Her Majesty's extraordinary originality and aesthetic sense. Sadly, the one I personally received was destroyed in the bombing during World War II. This is the one she gave the Prince, and it survived because it had been put away in the fireproof storehouse.

As is evident from the wish she embodied in her design for the *bonbonnière*, the Empress Dowager was deeply interested and concerned about Japan's future as a world power and her relations with other countries. Her Majesty's outlook was truly international and she took a keen interest in learning about conditions abroad and foreign culture. She was particularly interested in the life of British and other royalty. She had never been abroad, and it was an age without television, and not many sources of information, but nevertheless she was well-informed in a large variety of fields. I realize now more than ever what a remarkable person Her Majesty, the Empress Dowager, was.

Her knowledge included the latest French fashions, and it was she who designed all the formal wear for us princesses, even choosing the materials. She may have enjoyed doing this because she had no daughters of her own. She also may have enjoyed the freedom that was hers as Empress Dowager – denied her while Empress – of being able to invite whom she liked when she liked, for she often invited the Prince and me over for an informal chat.

So the Prince and I decided to invite Her Majesty to our residence one evening for a real English dinner. The dining table and chairs and dishes had all been brought back from England by the Prince, and all the dishes we served that night were typically English. She was delighted. So we repeated the invitation several times, including the Prince's two brothers, Prince Takamatsu and Prince Sumi, and these family gatherings were greatly enjoyed by all. When we went out to dinner there was always a great to do with police security, but between houses in the same compound, as ours were, one could slip backwards and forwards without any fuss at all. We often invited the Empress Dowager for a typical English tea as well, which she enjoyed tremendously.

I meant to write about the comfort and encouragement I used to derive from the Empress Dowager's *bonbonnière* whenever I felt sad and dejected, but happy memories have come tumbling out one after the other instead. Many were the times when I in my youth and inexperience committed the most dreadful blunders. I blush even now when I think of some of them. The first one was when we returned to Tokyo after the enthronement ceremonies and visited the Tama Imperial Mausoleum with Their Majesties. I should have ascertained carefully beforehand when and how many times I was expected to bow, but the Prince had assured me that all I needed to do was to copy him, which I did – only to hear someone's discreet chiding voice behind me, 'Since Your Highness is on the distaff side, you should have turned once more, stopped, and bowed. Remember to do so next time.'

I was cut to the quick. Moreover, I had no idea what was meant by 'the distaff side'. Later, back in my own room I remember how downcast and dejected I felt. And then, suddenly, the rose-pink cord on the drum-shaped confection box caught my eye, and shed a warm glow in my heart. It seemed to say: 'You've learned something today. Be thankful for that.' At times like that I would pick up the little *bonbonnière* and hold it in my hand, and it never failed to bring calmness and peace.

My second *faux pas* occurred four days later when I attended the Grand Military Review on the Yoyogi Parade Ground in which the Prince took part as Commander, Sixth Company, Third Infantry Regiment. This time it was the coat I wore. I had a rather nice leather coat I had brought back from America, where they were all the rage. Now they are fashionable in Japan, too, but nobody wore leather coats here then, and eyebrows were raised in considerable disapproval. Being mid-winter, and expecting the parade ground to be cold and windy, I, in my ignorance, had thought it was just the thing to wear. Realizing that I knew no better, I was let off quite easily, although in private I think I was considered quite hopeless. I tremble to think what the consequences would have been had I worn that coat wilfully in full knowledge of the facts.

The dear little silver drum was to comfort me again on another occasion. While the Prince was attending the Military Academy, he used to walk there every day accompanied by his aide, Colonel Honma, returning some time between half past four and a little after five. Long before we could hear the sound of their footsteps on the gravel path, I would join the staff lined up at the front entrance to greet them. If the Prince was not giving an audience to some ambassador, or if there was no dinner party that evening, or some palace ceremony, he would have a cup of tea and *anpan*, soft bread-rolls filled with bean jam. The Prince had a sweet tooth, and was particularly fond of them, and usually ate more than one, after which he naturally was not very hungry at dinner-time. He knew that, but just could not resist them.

I, however, have never been very fond of sweet things, nor do I think that adzuki-bean jam goes well with bread, so I never had any. Looking back now, I wish I had joined him occasionally and had one. How stupid I was!

Since I never touched the bean-jam rolls, the servants finally took to serving me little sandwiches, which, in my *naïveté*, I ate with relish.

And that, too, was apparently a dreadful thing to have done. I was severely reprimanded for being selfish and allowing myself to be served with something I enjoyed for tea instead of keeping His Highness company. They were right, of course. There was no excuse for my behaviour. This time I realized how thoughtless and insensitive I had been, and I dissolved into tears.

In Washington, although we often had an English-style four-o'clock family tea together, I was still considered a child and excluded from adult entertaining. Then I was suddenly thrust into court life without having even had any experience of ordinary Japanese social life. I think that was why I kept making so many mistakes.

It would have helped, perhaps, if I could have consulted my parents from time to time, but they were in far-away England. The telephone was not yet fully developed, and letters took forty days each way. Besides, I had been casually warned not to write too much of a private nature.

These were some of the many hurdles I have had to overcome.

MILITARY ACADEMY HOMEWORK

On 1 January 1929, I attended my first New Year's Day ceremony at the Palace. All the members of the Imperial Family were lined up in ceremonial dress in the corridor leading to the Grand Audience Chamber. Each of the princesses were provided with two train bearers – boys dressed as pages who had been selected from among the pupils of the Peers' School and meticulously rehearsed.

We proceeded to the Phoenix Room, where the members of the Imperial Family offered felicitations to Their Majesties. Then we followed Their Majesties to the Main Hall, where we stood in attendance at their side while dignitaries, as their names were called by the Grand Master of Ceremonies, came up in turn and offered felicitations to Their Majesties. After that, we proceeded on through three reception rooms receiving greetings from the people standing in rows therein. This continued until four o'clock, when we attended upon Their Majesties' departure. A similar ceremony took place the following day.

As for the New Year rituals at our own residence, our servants and ladies-in-waiting had all been previously trained in various other princely households so although I was a new Imperial bride I had nothing to worry about and could leave things to them. Incidentally, Senior Lady-in-Waiting Sagawa, who had been trained in Prince Takeda's household, was from Aizu. Looking back now, I realize how much both she and Lady-in-Waiting Yamaza must have done to shield me in my ignorance.

That year, it is recorded that 850 people came to our palace to offer New Year felicitations. We did not, of course, receive them all. Most of them simply wrote their names in the book. Relatives, intimate friends, and special persons, however, were invited inside and received by the Prince and me. I remember the Prince greeting at the entrance a large number of soldiers who had once served under him in the Third Infantry Regiment and had come to offer their New Year felicitations to us both.

New Year evenings were usually free, and we often played poem-card games. The Palace version – called the 'Noh card game' – was much more sedate than the usual 'Hundred Poems by a Hundred Poets', and simpler, provided one could read the difficult calligraphy peculiar to Noh chants and knew the plays in the Noh repertory. It was a good way to widen one's knowledge of the Noh, but many members of the Imperial family, such as young Prince Sumi, much preferred the more generally popular version of the game based on poems from the famous thirteenth century Hundred Poets Anthology of thirty-one syllable *tanka* – also known as *waka*.

It is a much livelier game. There are two decks of cards, one set bearing the first three lines of the poems and the other the final couplets. While one player, designated 'reader', intones each triplet in turn from his shuffled deck, the rest of the players compete in picking up the relevant couplet from the cards of the second deck, which have been shuffled and placed face upwards at random.

Their Majesties and the Empress Dowager invariably played Noh cards, and many was the time I was invited to her palace to partner the latter, but it was always 'A Hundred Poets' at our Residence. We used to invite Prince Takamatsu and Prince Sumi (later called Prince Mikasa) over for a game, and I would head a women's team of ladies-in-waiting, while the three princes would be joined by Chamberlain Watanabe. The rest of the male staff used to try and avoid playing poem cards, making all sorts of excuses, but Watanabe invariably got roped in.

The Prince was very good at Noh cards, but not having played Hundred Poets until my arrival, his team always lost. He was a keen competitor, and tried hard to memorize the poems, but being more experienced at the game I usually won. It was the only game in which I was able to beat him.

After taking part in the first military review of the year on 8 January 1929, the Prince began a busy schedule which combined studies at the military academy with his official duties as a member of the

Imperial Family.

He attended the academy for three years, during which time hardly a night went by without copious homework that had to be done. When there were no evening functions to attend, he would come home from the academy, have a leisurely tea, read the newspaper and seem so relaxed that I would think to myself, how lovely, he has no homework to do today. Then, after a leisurely dinner and another perusal of the newspapers, just when I was quite sure he had the evening free, he would settle down to his homework at about half past seven – and he would not finish until one or two in the morning, and sometimes even later than that.

Once in a while, some professor would come to the Residence after dinner to give the Prince a lecture, which usually lasted until eleven. And then there were the many diplomatic and other dinner parties we attended, when we did not get home until eleven-thirty. The Prince would begin his homework very late on those occasions, and always urged me to go on to bed, but somehow I could not bring myself to do so. Instead, I used to wait up for him in the Middle Room as it was called. This was the room between my sitting-room and the Prince's.

I realize now that it would have been sensible to snooze, but being young, it never occurred to me. Or I could have studied too. I could have read books, and practised the poetry and calligraphy required of a princess. But I was tired and sleepy after those parties and did not feel like studying. Although I was aware that the Prince was probably just as tired as I was, I simply whiled away the hours playing games I could play by myself, like Corinthian, a simple form of pinball popular then. Sometimes a member of the staff who happened to be on duty would keep me company. I tried to think of ways I could help my husband – but there was little I could do other than sharpen his pencils.

The Prince would ring for a cup of green tea after he had worked for about two hours, and I would think, ah, I'll be able to go to bed now. But no, he would drink his tea and begin work again. Sometimes he would come into the Middle Room and ask me to order the tea. Then I would really think, with relief, that his work was over, but I would be wrong again. He had just been taking a breather.

It went on like this night after night, followed by an early departure for the academy the following morning. He never even slept late on Sundays, but would be up by 8.30 am. Some nights he worked all night and did not get any sleep at all.

Shigesada Hayashi, a classmate of the Prince's at the academy, writes as follows in a biography of the Prince he compiled twenty years after the Prince's death.

> 'The difficult assignments we took home would often take us until one or two in the morning to complete, so when we read in the paper next morning that HIH Prince and Princess Chichibu had attended a dinner at the America-Japan Society or something like that, good heavens! we thought, and used to ask him what time he managed to finish his homework. He would often reply that he had not slept at all that night.
>
> One cold snowy Saturday afternoon after school was over, as I accompanied His Highness as far as the main road, I said 'Tomorrow's Sunday so we can take it easy for a change!' and he said he couldn't as he'd got to see some ambassador or other. I felt terribly sorry for him.'

I once remonstrated with him and said I thought he was working far too hard.

'There are lots of my classmates', he replied, 'who

have to do the same work in cramped quarters with an infant bawling its head off. Here am I working in quiet, palatial surroundings, so I've little to complain of.'

The quiet. I remember those nights of the Prince's military academy days as if it were yesterday. I remember the silence – made all the deeper by the occasional hoot of an owl or the cry of some other night bird in the great deodars and oak trees of the spacious garden.

After completing his courses at the military academy, the Prince continued his studies of poetry and calligraphy. As for me, with no basic training in these arts I was a mere beginner. Taneaki Chiba had given me a brief pre-marriage course in the composition of *waka*, but now I submitted my original poetic efforts to Koji Torino for correction. It embarrasses me now to remember how poor my early efforts were! All I tried to do then, as I remember, was to express my feelings, and I did not worry too much about the form.

I had hoped to have piano lessons, too, having never studied properly with a teacher. I could read music a little, and often after lunch the ladies-in-waiting would gather around the piano and we would sing some of the popular war and regimental songs. 'Blossoms at dawn' was a new favourite, and the words had been written by the Prince's aide-de-camp, Lieutenant-Colonel Honma.

As a matter of fact, the Prince had a hand in Colonel Honma's composition of the poem. Just about the time I arrived back from America, the Prince was taking part in a military exercise at the base of Mount Fuji and he had not allowed his aide to accompany him. This was because he wanted to be on the same footing as his fellow officers with no privileges accorded to him as an Imperial prince. Colonel Honma, therefore, having accompanied the Prince as far as the barracks at Takigahara, was obliged to wait there for twelve days with nothing to do and whiled away his boredown by composing an entry for a nationwide competition for the words to a new war song.

The announcement that Honma's entry had won came just after our wedding, and the Prince was overjoyed. The music, composed at the Military Band School in Toyama was very catchy, and the song was a great hit.

Colonel Honma had become the Prince's aide-de-camp at the instigation of the Empress Dowager, who expressed the hope that he would stay with the Prince in that capacity for a long time. The Prince had the fullest confidence in Colonel Honma's sincerity and faithfulness. The Colonel taught me and the ladies-in-waiting how to play bridge, and often played tennis with us, too. When he went away to London as Military Attaché in June, 1930, I regretted that I had not had him help me improve my English, as well. Few Japanese had as good a grasp of the language as he did. When the Prince and I attended King George VI's coronation in London in 1937, Colonel Honma was one of our suite, and towards the end of the Pacific War, just before his ill-fated departure for the Philippines, he made several visits to us to see the Prince, who was then ailing.

HIKING IN THE SUMMER HOLIDAYS

Not long ago, a former member of our staff came to visit me, and we had a great laugh together over the roller-skating the Prince and I used to indulge in at midnight.

'Your Highnesses used to do it,' he said, 'just when

we all thought you were asleep. It must have been a wonderful relaxation for His Highness to have that bit of exercise roller-skating in the upstairs corridors for a little while before turning in after studying all those hours. I remember how startled those of us downstairs were the first time. We thought it was thunder.'

Reminded of it sixty years later, I did not know at first whether to be embarrassed or to laugh! The former staff member went on to remind me how the Prince and I used to skate on our pond when it froze over in winter, and ski on the gentle slopes of the landscaped garden.

The Prince loved sports of all kinds, both to participate in and to watch. We had a tennis court, and we played together whenever the Prince could find the time, which was not very often. He also had a squash court built in the house with the help of someone from the British Embassy. It enabled him to take short amounts of exercise and work up a healthy sweat even on rainy days. Squash is played a lot in Japan now, but it was the Prince who first introduced the game to this country. He felt it was ideally suited to Japan.

Mountaineering was the Prince's favourite sport. He climbed the Matterhorn in the Swiss Alps while a student in England, and there is hardly a peak in Japan which he did not scale, from the Japanese Alps to the Chichibu Range from which he derived his title. Mountains gave him spiritual freedom and peace of mind, and he liked the discipline.

He took me with him once on a hike during one of his vacations from the military academy. Takeji Aso came along as our guide. I knew the Prince wanted to introduce me to the joy of mountain climbing, but to me it was far from a 'hike'. We started from Nikko and made our way over the Konsei Pass to Ikaho, where we spent the night. From there we climbed Mount Haruna, and then drove by car to Karuizawa. Next day, we walked all the way from Kanbayashi to Hoppo, and the day after that we climbed Mount Iwasuge, 2,295 metres above sea level.

As far as I was concerned it was a forced march. Although I had been a tomboy as a child, I had never walked in the hills. Moreover, I was not dressed properly for mountaineering. It was the hottest time of the year and the paths were dizzyingly steep. I only managed to finish the course by taking frequent rests. I began to wonder if being walked off one's feet was another of the requirements of a princess.

But the Prince had not been trying to make it an endurance test for me. It was only later I realized that not having any sisters, he had no idea what an ordeal it would be for me. I still remember how considerate he was on the way down. When we came upon a slope of slippery red earth, Mr Aso passed me his mountaineering stick and the Prince took hold of my other arm and together they helped me safely down.

Looking back, I think of that trip as our real honeymoon. Admittedly it was rough. There were no lights where we spent the night in Hoppo. But it was a trip I shall never forget as long as I live.

The Prince was a professional-class skier, having been coached by Kunio Igaya. And he used to scull in Hayama, where we had a summer villa. The Prince tried very hard to teach me to row but I was no good at it at all. It was such a shame, as he was so eager to have me experience the exhiliration of gliding through the sparkling blue ripples the way he did. The Prince loved taking part in all sports except boxing. Rugby was one of the sports he enjoyed watching most. But more about that later.

Just before I married Prince Chichibu, an Imperial Family Social Club had been formed, of which he had been one of the founders. Meetings were held once a month in a different princely house each time, and a speaker invited to lecture on some timely topic, after which there would be a pleasant get-together. There were so many aunts and cousins that sometimes there would just be games – the poem-card game if it were New Year – and dancing. The Prince was always the life and soul of the party.

We had film shows, too, since we were not able to go to the public cinema. The Empress Dowager often came to these. I remember how much we all enjoyed *Morrocco*, *The Merry Widow* and *Tom Sawyer*.

Besides taking a lively interest in so many things, I think the Empress Dowager missed not having had any daughters of her own. The spring following my marriage, she expressed a desire to see my Doll's Festival display, and came to see it every year.

# CHAPTER SEVEN

# *Our Daily Life*

A VISIT TO THE CHICHIBU MOUNTAINS

O n 4 February 1930, Prince Chichibu's younger brother Nobuhito, Prince Takamatsu, married Lady Kikuko Tokugawa. The Empress Dowager was, of course, delighted, and as for me, I was overjoyed to gain a royal sister-in-law, and she proved to be a great source of strength to me. Prince and Princess Takamatsu were always so helpful and kind to both of us over the years.

Prince Chichibu graduated from the military academy on 28 November 1931. People may imagine that Imperial princes attending the academy are invariably helped by their aides-de-camp in their studies and in the field exercises, but Prince Chichibu exploded that myth once and for all. Not only his aides – Colonel Honma, and later Colonel Okada – could attest to that fact, but every single one of his classmates.

At the graduation ceremony, the officer with the highest marks receives a sword from the Emperor. The

Prince's marks were not announced, but when he entered the academy, as a member of the 43rd Graduating Class, his academic record at first was disappointing. However, his marks rose higher and higher each year through his own dedicated efforts – all privilege and leniency having been strictly forsworn – so that he, too, received a sword from his brother, the Emperor.

On graduation, the Prince was appointed a Company Commander of the Third Infantry Regiment so his days continued to be full with his combined military and Imperial duties. It was just three months after the Manchurian Incident, and after an expeditionary First Division, which included sixty men from the Third Infantry Regiment, had made their obeisances in front of the Imperial Palace, the Prince saw them off at Tokyo Station. He had taken a fatherly interest in each of the men under him, and their families, so I know his heart ached to see them go.

I went to the Palace Plaza, too, in a private capacity, to see these brave men who were about to cross the sea for sovereign and country, and I hoped fervently that war would not spread in Manchuria.

On 8 April 1932, the Empress Dowager expressed a wish to see how ordinary soldiers lived, and made a tour of inspection to the barracks of the Third Infantry Regiment, in which I accompanied her. This kindly lady wanted the soldiers to know of her warm concern for them.

On 15 May, we returned home from attending a student field-and-track meet to find our residence bristling with policemen, guards and members of the Kempeitai. It seemed that there had been an attack on the homes of the Prime Minister and several other cabinet ministers. We were greatly alarmed, and the

Prince left immediately for the palaces of the Emperor and the Empress Dowager.

Following this dastardly affair, which became known as the 'Five-one-five Incident' from the date it took place, the Prince participated in a succession of marches and exercises, and owing to the serious and precarious national and international situation, he had little time now for sports, and on 1 September he was posted to the Second Operational Division, General Staff Headquarters.

Once again, as in his military academy days, the Prince would come home in the evenings and shut himself in his study until all hours – very often all night long. As for me, I could not help but worry about his health as I whiled away the time working on my poetry and calligraphy and doing embroidery.

The work he brought home from Headquarters concerned important operational plans which he would ponder thoroughly, going over them again and again. It was all highly secret, and so he had to do any mimeographing and hectographing himself.

On 15 August 1933, however, we made a six-day trip to the Chichibu Three Peaks and spent five nights at the summit Guest House. On the second day, after worshipping at Mitsumine Jinja, the celebrated Three Peaks shrine, we had intended to walk through the forest to the observation platform, but the fog was so heavy that both the Prince's hat and my parasol soon were wringing wet. Visibility was nil, so we returned to the Guest House and decided to make it a day of rest. But not for the Prince. As was invariably the case, he had brought along work to do. When he turned on a lamp at dusk, however, he was plagued by insects of every description.

The Prince had visited the Three Peaks shrine soon

after he was first made Prince of Chichibu in November 1922, and again when he was about to set off for England to study in 1925. This time it was because he wanted me to see 'his' mountain and to introduce me to the people of the district.

The mountain scenery was indeed beautiful, and the tall cryptomerias, with their tops hidden in the mists reminded me of Japanese paintings. The fourth day of our trip dawned fine and sunny, and we walked up to the observation point and then, after breakfast, we climbed Mount Myōhō. The mountain, whose contours stood out boldly that day against the clear autumn sky, had several sections that were very difficult to climb. Iron ladders had been affixed in some places, and in others, the wet rock faces were so slippery that one had to find footholds on old imbedded tree roots. Finally, there was an iron chain for hauling oneself up. My simple frock, ordinary walking shoes and staff did not help much as I frantically tried to keep up with my companions. The Prince, an experienced alpinist and rock-climber, had no trouble at all with the ladders and would be out of sight in no time, only to reappear from some hidden path to encourage me.

'Just hold on tight and you can do it. There's nothing to worry about!'

We reached the summit at last. Chichibu is famous for its fog and so there was no view, but we heard a beautiful burst of song from a bush-warbler somewhere down below the sea of mists, and on the way down, we flushed out the occasional pheasant and butcherbird. It was like being in an enchanted kingdom, far from the everyday world.

The next day we set off for Swallow Rock on Mount Shiraiwa's Jizō Pass. We could see craggy Mount

Myōhō on our left as we climbed through fields of alpine flora. It was a far gentler environment than that of the previous day. We sat down for a while among the wildflowers, and I particularly remember how lovely the columbines were.

We left Mount Mitsumine – Chichibu's Three Peaks – the following day, on the twentieth, and were given a warm send-off by the local people. Back in Tokyo, the Prince became caught up again in his busy schedule of military and Imperial duties, with hardly a moment to spare. Every Wednesday evening Professor Hiraizumi of Tokyo University came to lecture him on 'Japanese Political History' and I always joined in these sessions.

On 23 December 1933, an event long hoped-for by the nation came to pass – the birth of Crown Prince Akihito. The whole country celebrated this happy event with flag parades and lantern processions, and joy was universal. His birth was like a bright light that shed hope on a dark and foreboding period in Japan, when the future seemed so uncertain – a time of crop failures, economic panic, and undernourished children.

THE TEMPORARY IMPERIAL RESIDENCE, HIROSAKI

On 2 June 1934, not long after Pu Yi, the last Emperor of China, had been made Emperor of Manchukuo, the Prince, as the representative of his brother, the Emperor of Japan, made a trip to Changchun, the capital of Manchukuo, to carry a personal letter from His Majesty and to present Pu Yi with a decoration.

The following April, the Prince and I were at Yokohama to meet Emperor Pu Yi when he officially visited Japan, and we accompanied him to all the various functions, including tea with the Empress Dowager.

Then in August, the Prince was posted to the castle town of Hirosaki in Aomori Prefecture. Promoted to the rank of Major, he had been appointed Commander of the Thirty-first Infantry Regiment which had its headquarters in the extreme north of Honshū, Japan's main island. We left Tokyo together on 9 August 1935, by train.

The Prince had volunteered for a posting in the cold Northeast, since no member of the Imperial Family had ever been posted there before except for a brief sojourn by Prince Fushimi. My husband had actually asked for Hokkaido, but being only accessible by sea, Hokkaido was deemed impracticable in the event of an emergency which might call him back to Tokyo.

I believe the reason he wanted to go to such a cold region stemmed from his Third Regiment days, when most of the new recruits he trained came from poor homes in the 'East End' of Tokyo. Feeling responsible for these men, he would ask them about their living conditions, and when he discovered how wretched these usually were, he was appalled to think of how many people there were living in conditions so different from his own. I think that is why he wanted to experience for himself the harsh conditions of the cold northeast.

In actual fact, however, it turned out to be the most relaxed posting he could have chosen. There were no Imperial duties, so while he was quite busy with military duties he did not have to cope with the other and could enjoy to the full the pleasures of life in the country. If only he had been able to complete his two-year tour there, instead of having to cut it short after only a year-and-a-half, I think his health would have greatly benefited.

We lived in a house in Konya, outside Hirosaki,

belonging to a Mr. Kikuchi. While we were there it was known as the Temporary Imperial Residence. It was surrounded by rice fields, and we could watch all the aspects of rice culture as well as feasting our eyes of the lovely green of the young rice, waving in the breeze and stretching off into the distance beyond our windows,. Although we had only just arrived, we were soon hoping for a bumper crop along with the farmers, our neighbours. The Prince photographed the whole rice cycle from planting to harvest with his sixteen-millimetre movie camera, to show to the Empress Dowager. The Iwaki River flowed nearby, and its gentle murmur was most soothing. Hirosaki Castle, the seat of the feudal lords of the Tsugaru domain, was not far away, and from our upstairs windows we could see Mt. Iwaki and Mt. Hakkoda where we often took walks.

The Prince's private secretary and my ladies-in-waiting had come with us from Tokyo, but we had local cooks and maids, so there was plenty of direct contact with the people of the region – nice, relaxed people we found soothing to live amongst.

Winter comes early to Japan's snow country. Each day, after the Prince had left for Headquarters, I used to sit with my feet in the *kotatsu* – a table-topped quilt-covered framework over a charcoal brazier – and spend the time painting, or practising poetry. We also learned the local folksongs with their complicated melodies and refrains. I can still hear some of those lilting Tsugaru songs in my mind. Snowed in for days on end there was plenty of time to spare.

It also snowed in Tokyo, of course. Two years before we moved to Hirosaki, we once had five or six inches of snow in our garden and the Prince gave me my first skiing lessons on the garden slopes. But while the snow I was used to drifted down silently, the snow up north seemed to beat down mercilessly, with great thuds, quickly blotting out the landscape. Next morning, you would find snow had even forced its way in through the shutters.

Until quite recently, I used to receive quilted jackets from an elderly Hirosaki friend. They were in traditional Hirosaki *kogin* work – dark-blue homespun linen with geometric patterns stitched in amongst the weave in heavy white yarn. During the snowbound months the women used to make work clothes like this for themselves and their daughters' trousseaux – garments to last a lifetime. They were so beautiful we found it hard to believe they were only worn for work, but that was indeed their purpose – clothes to keep you warm while doing heavy work like sawing snow when the weather was coldest.

Snow shovelled off the roofs several times a winter to keep the weight down would pile up on the ground and become rock hard, eventually having to be sawed into blocks and carried away. On an appointed day at winter's end, each household was expected to clear the snow in front of their house. What a cheering sight it was to see the children playing ball on roads whose earthen surfaces had reappeared: one knew then that spring had come. The Prince no longer had to ski to brigade headquarters. After 'snow-sawing' he could make the four-kilometer trip by car.

On 24 December, when we had been at Hirosaki four-and-a-half months, the Prince was given a fort-night's holiday so we both went down to Tokyo to attend my brother Ichirō's wedding. After paying our respects at the Palace we called upon the Empress Dowager, who was delighted to hear all about our life in the Tsugaru region. She had been concerned about our going to such a cold place, and had enjoined us to be careful about our health, so she was especially relieved to see the Prince looking so well. She expressed pleasure to see that it had apparently agreed with me, too.

Besides visiting the Mausoleum at Tama, we managed to attend a meeting of the Imperial Family Social Club. It was nice seeing everyone again, and there was much to talk about. My father's tour of duty as Ambassador in London had ended in August, and he was back in Japan, so my parents were able to be at my brother's wedding on the twenty-seventh.

We took the night train back to Hirosaki before New Year's week was up, arriving in a blizzard, so that the Prince could be back in time for the first review of the year on 8 January. Busy days of military duties followed. But on Sundays, we went skiing in the foothills of Mount Sasamori. Though still a learner, I was beginning to enjoy the sport and practised dilligently, longing to be good enough to accompany the Prince to more advanced slopes. I do not think we ever had more time to ourselves than in those Hirosaki days.

The coldest time of the year in Hirosaki began about the middle of January, with blizzards almost every day, makng driving impossible so that the Prince had to ski to work most of the time. But it was in good health and high spirits that he participated in night skiing exercises, reviewed the Thirty-second Infantry Regiment (Yamagata Corps), and took part in a cold-weather endurance march involving a two-night bivouac. I went too when he inspected the Ski Corps in Owani. We stayed overnight there, and for me the opportunity to meet more local people was a joy.

And then there was one morning I shall never forget.

It must have been two or three days after we returned to Hirosaki from Owani. There had been a blizzard the day before, and the morning sun was dazzling as it sparkled on the snow. It was the day of the 'Two-two-six Incident' in Tokyo, so-called because it took place on the twenty-sixth day of the second month – February, 1936.

There had been a telephone call from Prince Takamatsu early in the morning, and I sensed something was wrong. 'Nothing to worry about,' my husband replied when I asked him about it, and left for duty as usual. Radio news was censored in those days, and long-distance telephone calls took hours to put through. Various rumours reached us around noon, but the staff and I only had a vague idea about what had happened. We were on tenterhooks all day.

The Prince left for Tokyo late that night. A second telephone call had come through from his brother in the afternoon, asking him to come, and his private secretary had gone to regimental headquarters to relay the message. Some junior officers leading a large number of soldiers had taken control of central Tokyo and assassinated several cabinet ministers. The Emperor was determined to quell the insurrection, and Prince Takamatsu decided his brothers should assist him in doing so. My husband already knew from the morning telephone call of His Majesty's anger and had been planning to go to Tokyo as soon as possible.

The Prince's anger, too, knew no bounds. He could not condone the act of the rebel officers in using national military forces to try to further their own ideas, killing and injuring a large number of people in the process. The Emperor welcomed him warmly and together with the Empress, entertained him to dinner that night.

The Prince telephoned me once but did not give me any details. Again, all he said was not to worry. Eventually I read in the newspaper about the insurrection and that it had been successfully put down. I was greatly relieved, but the Prince was away such a long time I could not help feeling uneasy.

He returned on 9 March and left immediately for regimental headquarters. When he came home that night he told me he had seen my parents and they were well. I was extremely touched by his thoughtfulness. He also told me something I did not know. When the new Hirota cabinet had been formed after the 'Two-two-six Incident', I had read in the newspaper that my father had been appointed Imperial Household Minister, but I was unaware that he had declined at first and that his refusal had been overruled.

By the end of March, the Prince had managed to clear up the backlog of work that had accumulated while he was in Tokyo, and every Sunday we went to Mount Sasamori to ski.

Spring comes late to the snow country and the cherry blossom season is not until the middle of May. The blossoms surrounding the old manor house and the vermillion-lacquered bridge over the moat are breathtakingly beautiful. We often joined the crowds that flocked to see them. Sometimes we went to see them at night, and when the petals began to fall, the pale pink 'blizzards' as they swirled down into the moat were also very beautiful.

In June, we picked edible bracken shoots on Mount Iwaki, and in August there was the five-day Neputa festival for which Hirosaki is famous. Now Aomori Prefecture has turned the festival into a large-scale show, with big, elaborate floats, but in those days, the displays were small affairs – handmade paper models of every description, with candles inside, which would be carried about the town from house to house from dusk until midnight to the sound of fifes and drums. They also used to bring them around to our Temporary Imperial Residence. Then on 7 August, the last day of the festival, the models were set adrift on the Iwaki River to the accompaniment of a special song. It was all quite fairylike as the models drifted along, their inner candles flickering. There was an indescribable sadness about it, too, as one savoured the emotions peculiar to the region.

In addition to these peaceful pursuits, the Prince worked hard at his military duties, conducting overnight bivouacs and protracted military exercises, as well as umpiring war games. Once he even had to stand for hours on the summit of Mount Iwaki in the middle of the night in the rain. The result of their training was plainly evident in the special exercises in Hokkaido in October, where the Hirosaki Thirty-first Regiment won first place and high commendation, which pleased the Prince immensely.

Very soon after that, we received word from the Imperial Household that we were to proceed to England, and so, on 7 November, I accompanied the Prince to the Palace to wait on His Majesty's command.

ATTENDING THE CORONATION

Britain's King George V had died and was succeeded by the Prince of Wales, who became King Edward VIII, and was to be crowned in May, 1937. We were to attend the coronation as representatives of the Emperor and Empress. To enable us to prepare for the trip, it was decided that the Prince should be transferred to First Division, Army Staff Headquarters in Tokyo on 1 December.

In the meantime, as a result of what became known as the love affair or the century, the new king abdicated on 11 December, and his brother the Duke of York succeeded to the throne as King George VI. The Coronation, however, proceeded according to schedule.

When we left Hirosaki on 7 December, we left part of our hearts there. Although we had not been able to stay for the full two years, it was our first experience of living in the country, and we loved the warmth and simple kindness of the people.

We sailed for England on 18 March 1937, on the *Heian Maru*, with a suite of eleven that included the Grand Master of Ceremonies, Chief Lady-in-Waiting Yamaza and two others. After crossing Canada by train, we embarked on the luxury liner *Queen Mary* from New York. To be in America again nine years after I had been at school there filled me with nostalgia, and most moving of all, we were met by the Japanese aeroplane *Divine Wind* which had flown to New York to greet us after its ninety-two-hour flight from Tokyo to London. When he heard they were coming, the Prince had worried that they would not be able to see where we were on the deck and devised the following plan. He had the ladies-in-waiting sew a red circle – cut from some scarlet damask I happened to have with me – onto a white sheet, and when the *Divine Wind* appeared in the sky we spread it out for them to see. It was a great success. Pilot Iinuma and his engineer, Tsukakoshi, in their tiny low-wing monoplane, circled the part of the ship where we stood, over and over again. I thought of Lindbergh's *Spirit of Saint Louis* as the Prince and I waved to them.

We arrived at Southampton the evening of 12 March

and were greeted by Japanese Ambassador Shigeru Yoshida, after which we were conducted on board the battleship *Queen Elizabeth* by Admiral of the Fleet Sir Dudley Pound for dinner and to stay overnight.

Next day, we went by special train to London, where the Duke of Gloucester met us at the Hyde Park Hotel. It was eleven years since the Prince and the Duke had met, and they greeted one another like old friends. As for me, since I had left London only eight months after my birth there, everything should have seemed quite new, but curiously, everything seemed strangely familiar.

Our days, before and after the Coronation on 12 May, were filled with all sorts of engagements, both private and official, and what with the Prince renewing his acquaintance with people he had known while at Oxford University, every minute seemed to be taken up, and there was little time left for rest and relaxation.

The very first person the Prince wanted to see was Major General Laurence Drummond, (Ret'd.), at whose home he had lived while studying in England, and who had looked after him so kindly. The General was greatly moved to see the Prince again after eleven years and to receive the gift he had brought from his mother, the Empress Dowager.

After we had moved from the Princess Hotel in Hove to the more central Hyde Park Hotel in London, I accompanied the Prince to see some of his favourite rugby, and we also went for walks in the area around Kenley House on Kingston Hill where he had lived with the Drummonds.

On 11 May, the Prince made a nostalgic visit to Oxford, his *alma mater*, to receive an honorary degree from the University together with Paul, Prince Regent of Yugoslavia. I treasure the photograph taken then of the Prince in his academic gown. He looks so young, so healthy, and so handsome. It is so apparent in that photograph how that was the time in his life that he was the most fulfilled, both spiritually and physically.

Rather than giving my own faltering impressions of the Coronation, I shall quote from the Prince's 'Memories of England'.

'Sixty-three countries were represented among the guests at Westminster Abbey for the Coronation. The ceremony itself was both solemn and magnificent. There was no-one who was not intensely moved, after the two hour rites were over – three hours in King George V's day – when, to the strains of the national anthem, the king left the hall with quiet dignity.

The climax of the ceremony was the moment of crowning. The Archbishop of Canterbury says, "May God crown thee with honour and right-eousness" as he places the crown on the sovereign's head, at which moment all the members of royalty and the nobility put on their coronets. There is a shout of "God save the King!" and a salute is fired at the Tower of London. The royal and noble ladies put on coronets, too, together with the Queen Consort. Up until then, the king has been sitting in King Edward's Chair below the altar, but now he sits on the throne for the first time and the Archbishop of Canterbury says: "From now on, in the name of God and the power and majesty thou hast been given as king and emperor, may thou maintain it with all thy power."

The Archbishop of Canterbury, followed by the other bishops, then kneel before the king and swear their allegiance, followed by his two younger brothers and representatives of all the peerage.'

There was just one thing that bothered the Prince

about the ceremony. It was the fact that only the nobility seemed to have been invited to witness this once-in-a-lifetime ceremony for a beloved monarch, and that no representatives of the people took part. But he came to the conclusion that with their deep regard for tradition, the people were satisfied that it should be that way. There was no sign of class dissatisfaction or jealousy, and the people lining the route were at one in their hearts with the people in the Abbey.

As representatives of Their Majesties the Emperor and Empress of Japan, the Prince and and I were happy to find that we were always given precedence over the representatives of the other nations. There was no advance notice of the order of precedence, but when the day came, we discovered that our carriage headed the cavalcade of guests, as did our seat in Westminster Abbey and at all the other functions afterwards. At the state banquet at Buckingham Palace the Prince led the Queen in to dinner and sat on her right, while I went in on the arm of the King's younger brother, the Duke of Gloucester, and sat on the left of the King. The Japanese Imperial Family was treated with especial respect by the British Royal Family. Whatever the reason, the extraordinary friendliness expressed to us by the British Royal Family was quite remarkable.

When the Prince was studying in England, King George V and Queen Mary invited him often to an informal family lunch, and the king gave him a pair of diamond cuff-links. He also learned to know the Prince of Wales quite well, too, and as it happened, he had the same rooms at Oxford that the Prince of Wales had used.

When Prince and Princess Takamatsu visited England after their marriage, and were having a private lunch at Buckingham Palace, to Princess Takamatsu's initial bewilderment, the very young Princess Elizabeth asked her, 'How is Ichiro?'. She was enquiring, it seems, after my young brother, and I was delighted to hear from the Takamatsus on their return to Japan how popular my family had been with the British Royal Family when my father was Ambassador in London.

When we attended the Coronation, it was in the interim period before the Manchurian Incident had escalated into the Sino-Japanese War, and world feeling towards Japan was not especially cordial, and the fact that Japan had signed an accord with Germany must have affected British feelings. That the Royal Family should have treated us so warmly at such a time touched us deeply.

After the Coronation was over, the Prince still kept to an energetic schedule, even going on to a ball at Buckingham Palace after a dinner hosted by Foreign Secretary Anthony Eden. I accompanied him to the ball given by the Duchess of Sutherland, which was attended by the King and Queen and Queen Mary, the Queen Mother, and I enjoyed it very much. The Prince was a good dancer, easy to follow. His English manners were impeccable, and he was very much at ease and popular with everyone.

On the nineteenth, we presented a letter and a decoration from the Emperor to the King at Buckingham Palace. The following day we watched a naval review at Portsmouth from on board the battleship HMS *Queen Elizabeth*, and visited the Japanese cruiser *Ashigara*, which was taking part. But whenever there was any time in between official duties, we would take the opportunity to enjoy the freedom we could never have at home. The Prince rode horseback in Hyde Park, and I joined him in going to the opera, the cinema, and shopping. There were no police escorts, and we felt like caged birds that had been set free.

Once, when the Prince was in a shop buying a gramophone, the assistant handed us a record with no label on it, saying, 'What about this as well?' We were mystified. It turned out to be a recording of King Edward VIII's abdication speech! To think that those unforgetably moving words with which the monarch of the great British Empire had given up his throne for love – that speech which was the culmination of the drama of the century, each single word of which resounded with pathos – to think that it had become a commercial commodity! We were shocked.

Ever since arriving in London we had taken such care to avoid the subject of the abdication. And here was this record blatantly on sale in a shop! After his initial amazement, however, the Prince was pleasantly amused at this new side of the British character which he had not seen before. In fact, he bought the record as a memento of his friend, and brought it back to Japan, where he listened to it several times.

In spite of the lovely June weather, I caught a cold, which kept me in for several days, and no sooner had I begun to recover than the Prince came down with one, so we had to miss the King's Birthday celebrations. Then no sooner was he well enough to take a walk than I became ill again, this time with pneumonia, requiring the services of two nurses.

But from then on until 8 July the Prince insisted on carrying out his full schedule of engagements without a single day's respite, in spite of not having fully recovered from his cold, since there was no-one to take his place. As for me I was distraught at not being able to help him at all.

It had been His Majesty the Emperor's wish that we travel to Europe after Britain, but cables had to be hurriedly sent to the Kings of Norway and Sweden sending our regrets and cancelling our visits there.

On 7 July, the Marco Polo Bridge incident in Peking took place, followed by a cease-fire agreement on the eleventh. But although the situation seemed to be under control, we were, in fact, already bogged down in a Sino-Japanese war.

Thankfully, I was finally well enough to get up, and prepare to travel to Switzerland on the fourteenth, where I was able to recuperate until the end of the month at a hotel in Grindelwald. Here, at an altitude of 1038 metres, the invigorating air and the views of the sparkling snow-capped alpine peaks not only restored our health but brought back happy memories to the Prince of the ascents he made of the Jungfrau and Wannehorn while on vacation in 1926.

We made the most of this carefree time devoid of official engagements. There were glaciers merely a short stroll away, and many were the picnics we enjoyed in the sunshine, among the gaily coloured wild alpine flowers, soothed by the tinkle of cowbells. One glacier had been hollowed out and contained an ice-rink,where we skated – an unforgettable memory. I remember how amazed we were by the iciness of a stream that flowed all the way down from the glacier to the village. Each day I felt better, and the Prince even felt up to visiting the League of Nations and the International Labour Organization in Geneva, as well as a clock factory.

After our fortnight's recuperation, we finally set off for the rest of our European tour. We arrived at the Hague on 2 August, attending a luncheon hosted by the Queen of the Netherlands on the third. We were invited to dinner that night with Princess Juliana and Prince Bernhardt, but my cold flared up again and I had to take to my bed, so the Prince went alone. But alas, he too took to his sick bed on returning.

It was obvious that to continue the tour would be not only a worry to Their Majesties the Emperor and Empress and the Empress Dowager, but to a great many other people involved as well. It was decided, therefore, to cancel the rest of the European tour and return to Japan as soon as our health would permit after some further recuperation in Grindelwald, which we finally left, reluctantly, about the middle of September. I went to London to await the Prince, who first paid a visit to Germany.

It was the Army's idea that he should go there, as the German-Japanese Anti-Comintern Pact had just been formed, and they felt it would boost relations with their new ally to have a Japanese prince pay them an official visit. The Prince attended a lunch given by Hitler at Nuremberg Castle, at which the Fuhrer launched a vitriolic verbal attack on Stalin, saying how much he hated him, in reply to which, the Prince retorted: 'Is it not wrong to express such prejudice against the Head of State of another country?' The Prince's candour disconcerted Hitler considerably, the Japanese ambassador, Kintomo Mushanokōji, gleefully noted.

Two or three days after the Prince joined me back in London we embarked at Southampton bound for home via Canada, arriving in Yokohama on 15 October. We had been away for seven months.

The Prince was clearly tired from the trip, but the political situation being what it was, he reported to the General Headquarters on the eighteenth to assume duty in Section Two of the Operational Planning Department.

# CHAPTER EIGHT

# *Up to the Outbreak of War*

---

## PAPIER MÂCHÉ STRING

*T*he Prince could not seem to get rid of the cough he had had ever since London, and even though his attending physician said he should rest for at least a month, the Sino-Japanese War had begun and he felt he could not take any leave. Numerous X-rays were taken, but we were told later that the condition of his lungs had been difficult to observe because of thickened scar tissue on the pleura resulting from an early illness.

Soon after returning home, I had gone down to our villa in Hayama for a change of air to rid myself of the lingering traces of my bout with pneumonia in London. To my relief, the Prince finally was able to join me for a spell at the beginning of December, although I doubt he had any peace of mind because of the hard-line policy towards England being advocated by the Army in the controversy between the military, politicians and diplomats of how to bring the Sino-Japanese war to a conclusion before it escalated. The Prince was the

Honorary Patron of the Japan-British Society, and through his knowledge of both England and America he was convinced that to break off friendly relations with those countries would only lead to Japan's ruin. Also, at this critical time, it pained him that the Army and the Navy did not see eye-to-eye.

News of the fall of Nanking reached us in Hayama.

The Prince returned to Tokyo before the New Year, but although I had fully recovered my health by about the middle of January, I stayed on in Hayama for another reason. The attending physician and I both thought that if I were in Hayama, the Prince would at least come down there for the week-ends, which would help towards the recovery of his health. Just as I expected, he did indeed join me every Sunday, and Saturdays when possible. I do not know how much of a help it was. There is no doubt that it gave him much-needed rest and recreation, but at a time when the root of his illness should have been thoroughly eradicated, I am now filled with remorse at my insufficient knowledge about his illness and the way I just kept harping on Hayama.

During this time the peace negotiations being negotiated by Germany between Japan and China were broken off and the Government broke off relations with Chang Kai-Shek and the war with China became a prolonged conflict.

That year, 1938, in March, the Prince was appointed Lieutenant-Colonel in the Infantry, and promoted to Colonel in August the following year. The pressure of work at the General Headquarters became extremely hectic. A long tour of duty in Manchuria was followed by analyses of each battle after continuously exhausting all-night observation of the battles standing on the bridge of the cruiser *Yura*. Most people would try and spare themselves as much as possible, but not the Prince. He was so dedicated, so conscientious. Truly a man of undiluted integrity. Being like that, he had always driven himself hard, even before entering the military academy, and now in spite of continued ill health, so that ultimately he succumbed to a disease he was unable to overcome.

And I kept on believing only that all the Prince needed was sufficient rest. In July 1938 we went up to Hakone to stay at Baron Fujita's mountain villa in Kowakidani. Again, I remained there all through August so the Prince could join me whenever he had a few days leave. He seemed so well on these occasions – except for his nagging cough.

Back at General Headquarters in Tokyo, when he was not on manoeuvres, he was never home until after dark, even in Summer when days were long. The building was old, and Colonel Kumao Imoto wrote of the unhealthy conditions of the sunless Operations room in which the Prince worked:

'His Highness, just like the other members of the staff, always worked until late in the dimly lit inner room, sitting straight upright maintaining correct military posture. He did everything himself, never delegating any of his duties to men under him. He was not very good at making those pieces of papier maché string you had to use at that time to hold one's papers together at the corners, and sometimes his were a bit clumsy. Once, without thinking, I offered to help him make his. With due respect, thinking back to those days, it seems to me that the unhealthy environment in which we worked was partly responsible for under-mining His Highness's health.'

Such work conditions were undoubtedly bad for the Prince's health, but the real cause lay in the strain he constantly subjected himself to in those working years as he strove to carry out both his Imperial duties and his military duties with a high degree of excellence, even when he himself was aware that his physical strength was far from up to it. That desire stemmed from the humility he felt regarding his upbringing as a member of the Imperial Family which was so vastly different from that of the poor army recruits. That is why, even when he let his men rest for an hour while on manoeuvre, he would not even allow himself to sit down. And during a cross river 'attack' at night in mid-winter, if someone had to lead the men into the cold muddy water, it was always he who would assume the rigorous task himself.

Now as I re-read Colonel Imoto's words, I picture the Prince at the War Office struggling with the unfamiliar task of rolling his own papier maché string to fasten the pages of his reports, and it blends in my mind's eye with the memory of one of those same hands ceremonially taking the hand of the Queen at Buckingham Palace.

THE ANTI-TUBERCULOSIS ASSOCIATION

The Prince and I spent a weekend together at our Hayama villa at the end of January, 1939. but soon after that he left Japan in connection with the attack on Canton. He lived aboard a warship for some time, and after returning to Japan he was so busy with official duties and observing manoeuvres that he was not able to take time off in Hayama again for quite a while. I stayed on at the seaside until April, still obsessed with the conviction that I could thereby induce him to join me whenever possible.

One day in May, Hidetada Hirose, the Welfare

Minister, called on me to ask if I would agree to become President of a proposed new organization to be called the Anti-Tuberculosis Association. He told me that my name had been suggested by Her Majesty the Empress, whose desire it was that I take on the job. Of course I said yes.

Earlier, the Empress had summoned the Prime Minister, Kiichiro Hiranuma, to the Palace on 28 April, where she had expressed satisfaction that something was being done for the prevention and cure of tuberculosis and handed him a personal contribution of five hundred thousand yen.

When we were at Hirosaki I had heard from the Prince of the large number of men in the army suffering from tuberculosis. Many of the soldiers there came from impoverished farming villages in Iwate Prefecture. Already suffering from malnutrition, the rigours of their training caused many to develop the disease.

Not only soldiers in Hirosaki but people all over Japan were succumbing to tuberculosis in increasing numbers every year as a result of malnutrition. Although the government was anxious to do something about this, counter-measures were inadequate, what with the military budget so stretched by the escalating war.

I knew nothing about the disease, but began to study material I obtained from the Association, wondering what there was that I could do to help in its prevention.

I read that in 1936 a total of 145,160 people had died – one tenth of those with the disease. It meant that of the entire population, one in fifty had contracted tuberculosis. What is more, these figures were three years old. One could assume that both the numbers who had died and the numbers who had contracted the disease – mostly young people in their teens and twenties – were now even greater. In Tokyo alone, the possibility of students and school children showing a positive reaction to a tuberculin test falling ill as a result of their environment was more than fifty percent. It was horrifying. It was no longer a question of whether I could be of any help. I was stirred into action. I simply *had* to do something.

Further study revealed that in Europe and America such strides had been made in the prevention and cure of tuberculosis that the numbers of both cases and deaths had been halved. While in Japan, facilities for the prevention and treatment of the disease were very poor. If things went on like that, cases would just go on increasing.

The means for the prevention of tuberculosis had, in fact, been in existence here since 1919. X-ray examination and tuberculin testing was available, but so much of the national budget had been allocated to defence that this important counter-measure had not been adequately taken, and had been left to the private sector to deal with.

The Japan Anti-Tuberculosis Association had been founded by the internationally known doctor Shibusaburo Kitazato, and included groups such as The White Cross Society, organized on Christian principles by a group of doctors, and Kazuo Tanabe's 'Nature Cure Society'. Depending precariously on donations alone, they did their best to try and stem the ferocious onslaught of the disease. On one hand there were the scientists carrying on their research, and on the other these private citizens fighting alone against great odds, until finally the government got around to doing something at last. The Department of Health within the Ministry of Home Affairs had managed to secure 100,000 yen to organize prevention measures, and just as it was on the point of being made a separate Welfare Ministry to grapple with tuberculosis, Her Majesty the Empress made her gift of 500,000 yen. This provided a great impetus, and the Cabinet immediately held a meeting and granted the Anti-Tuberculosis Association a state subsidy. The formal inauguration took place on 22 May 1939.

On the 30th, the Prince and I were received in audience by Their Imperial Majesties, and when I assured the Empress that I would do my very utmost to repay her trust in me, she must have felt my lack of confidence, for she smiled most kindly and, nodding, replied: 'I know you will do your best.' I was 29. I may have been the President in name, but I felt then that the true Head of the Anti-Tuberculosis Association was Her Majesty.

What with two weeks in Manchukuo and north China in June, followed by a spell at the front in central China in November, once again the Prince was too busy to take any time off. The day after his return from central China he resumed work straight away at the Staff General Headquarters in addition to his Imperial duties.

The ceremony inaugurating me as President of the Anti-Tuberculosis Association was held at the Tokyo Kaikan on 20 September. I sat on a dais before a gold screen, flanked by dignitaries, and read a message from Her Majesty the Empress. It was indeed a brilliant ceremony, and I was deeply moved to think that a movement started by the people, with faltering steps, should finally have attained this high government recognition. The eradication of tuberculosis was now no longer just a dream!

After I had read Her Majesty's message, there were speeches by the Chairman, Prime Minister Nobuyuki

Abe, and my father, who was the Imperial Household Minister.

That December, the Prince and I attended a dinner at my father's official residence. The Prince was relaxed and seemed to enjoy himself, and I was immensely happy to be able to spend an evening with my parents, something I had not been able to do for some time. The only sadness was that 'Taka' Takahashi was not there. Taka had died that March from a stroke, on the eve of her fifty-eighth birthday.

## THE PRINCE FALLS ILL

1940 was said to be the 2,600th year of the Imperial reign, and the Prince was appointed President of the commemmorative celebrations to be held in November. But in mid-June, he was obliged to take to his bed with a cold. Then, before he had completely recovered, he had to visit the Shrine at Ise to report on his appointment, as well as performing other duties, returning to Tokyo on the 20th and reporting to Their Majesties on the following day. That night he developed a fever. It proved to be the start of a long illness.

It was thought at the time to be bronchitis, and on 29 July he was considered well enough to be allowed up to attend at court for two days, and on 1 August we went up to the Fujita villa in Hakone for a change of air. The Prince was free of any temperature for two or three days, and enjoyed walks around the estate, but presently, his temperature rose and remained high. For the first time, the palace physicians diagnosed it as pulmonary tuberculosis. They informed the Prince, and ordered a complete course of medical treatment. It is impossible to put into words the emotional shock it was to me. And I could not possibly allow any of this to show. 'Pull yourself together' I kept telling myself. Although I tried to look calm, I was overcome by remorse and the feeling that I had somehow let the Prince down.

Among the material I had read on being appointed President of the Anti-Tuberculosis Association was an article headed 'The Importance of Early Detection'. At the time I had had a sort of uneasy feeling about the Prince's cough, since the symptoms sounded similar. But on his regular medical examinations they never discovered any lesions, so I decided my fears were groundless and faintheartedly said nothing, preferring to look on the bright side.

But it was no use chiding myself. I realized the most important thing I could do now was concentrate on helping the Prince have the best treatment to make him well.

The medical staff was headed by the Emperor's chief physician, Dr Hatta and the Army's Dr Nakamura, as well as Dr Endo, director of the Manchurian Railway's South Manchuria Sanatorium, well-versed in the treatment of TB, who was brought to Japan to head the team. Nurse Fumi Kawabe was brought in from the Red Cross Hospital.

The first thing prescribed by Dr Nakamura and Dr Endo was rest, both physical and mental. The Prince was made to realize that he must give up his overcrowded schedule and resign himelf to a prolonged period of medical treatment. He handed over his duties as President of the 2,600th Anniversary Ceremonies to his brother Prince Takamatsu, and moved down to Hayama from Hakone to begin his life of treatment in earnest, realizing he had no alternative.

He became a model patient, characteristically concientious and thorough in this as in everything else. During the twelve years of his struggle with the disease, never once did he entertain any lack of confidence in his phyisicians, trusting them completely. Even when his condition took some new turn, he would simply listen to the doctor's explanation and reply, 'I see', never asking for more details, and never questioning the treatment. Should the doctor suggest an operation, he would always agree. If no progress seems to be made over a long period, some think of changing doctors or hospitals, but the Prince never once wavered, always faithfully following doctor's orders. He was consistent in this to the very end. Indeed, pitifully so, I have sometimes thought.

In my studies I had read that there were two methods of treatment for TB. Neither of them were cures, since at that time the disease was considered incurable, but depended on whether the lesion had become a cicatrice or calcified, whether the bacillus had spread through the bronchi and veins. The aim was to prevent it from breaking through the membranes and spreading.

One method was called the 'general whole-body treatment' and consisted of keeping the patient quiet in a clean atmosphere and building up his strength with proper nutrition. The other method, called 'specialized treatment', involved any of the following: chemotherapy, atrophia, or 'direct treatment'. As for chemotherapy, streptomycin had not yet been discovered, and there was no effective drug, while atrophia involved pneumothorax or thoracoplasty to close the focus of the lesion in order to stop the activity of the bacilli. The 'direct treatment' involved completely taking out the vomica, which is the source of progress of the tuberculosis, and the lesion which will become aggravated sooner or later, but at that time Japan lacked the expertise, the facilities and the equipment to do this.

The method chosen by the Prince's doctors was the generalized treatment. He was only 38 when stricken by the disease, and if only streptomycin had been discovered, he would most certainly have recovered.

## A ROOM WITH A VIEW OF MOUNT FUJI

At the beginning of summer, after six months of convalescence at the seaside, in Hayama, the Prince became feverish again, and it was thought that perhaps the less humid air of the mountains would be better for him. The foothills of the Japan Alps, where there was a sanatorium, was considered, but would be too far from Tokyo for the doctors to commute by train. Gotemba was finally chosen. Although the air was not particularly dry, it was clean, and the winters were cold but the summers cool, and there was a fine view of Mount Fuji and Mount Ashitaka. It also met the important criterion of being within a day's commuting distance of Tokyo.

We heard that Count Kabayama wished to sell his villa there. I had spent every summer there as a child and knew it well. It was large, had two storeys, and we would be able to put up visitors. It faced south, and was just what we needed in every way.

Except for one thing. I had a feeling that the Prince would be bedridden for some time, and thought how wonderful for him it would be to be able to see Mount Fuji from his bed. And I remembered, alas, that at the Kabayama's one had to go outside in order to view the mountain. So we finally settled on a villa belonging to Junnosuke Inouye, and moved there from Hayama on

16 September 1941. Being wartime, petrol was unavailable, and cars had to run on charcoal. One was apt to have numerous breakdowns, but we managed the trip comfortably, without incident.

All 18 of us, including secretaries, nurses, maids, and kitchen staff, settled in at what came to be called the Prince Chichibu Imperial Villa, Gotemba. The house was situated in a forest on the left of the road from Gotemba to Hakone, and the trees were beginning to turn colour. The air was chilly but redolent of mountain freshness, and I sensed the Prince's satisfaction.

The house was a wooden bungalow with a thatched roof, and in addition to a spacious Western-style living-room, there were several Japanese-style rooms with tatami matting, and before we moved in an annex was built, joined to the main house by a corridor, with a large, comfortable combined bed-sitting-room and study for the Prince.

Almost all the rooms had a view of Fuji, the Prince could gaze at the mountain from morning till night, enjoying its varied aspects even as he lay in bed.

The mountain air agreed with the Prince, and he seemed so happy in the mountain villa that his temperature finally returned to normal, and by October, he was well enough to go down the veranda steps and walk a little in the garden.

On 18 October came the announcement that Hideki Tōjō had formed a new cabinet and would also be acting as Minister of Defence. I am quite sure the Prince did not feel the policy being advocated by the Army was good for the country, and now that he was relieved of his duties at General Headquarters he accepted his retirement with resignation and without regret.

On the 22nd, the Prince's younger brother, Takahito

Mikasa, married the lovely Yuriko, second daughter of Viscount Masanori Takagi, and I attended the ceremony alone. I had known him since he was a boy, when he had been known as Prince Sumi. He was now an officer in the Army and led a busy life, often visiting the front line. We were all very happy for him and wished them a long and happy life together.

On the 27th, my father, in his capacity as Imperial Household Minister, came with my mother to call on the Prince, who received my father in the study while my mother came to my room so I could ask her about the family. There was so much we wanted to say to one another, but we did not know where to begin. In the end we just talked about Mount Fuji and the birds that came to the garden.

The Minister was relieved to find the Prince looking so well, and after I had shown my parents around the house, they left.

The days that followed were without incident, and most days the Prince sat outdoors in the autumn sunshine from about 9 o'clock until noon. He weighed 154 pounds, and life seemed peaceful and quiet.

November brought with it severe winter weather. Mount Fuji grew whiter each day, with snow. I prayed that the Prince's first winter here would have no adverse effects upon his condition.

At about that time, Prince and Princess Takamatsu paid us their first visit, which we had looked forward to eagerly.

'What on earth have you done to your hands?' said the sharp-eyed Princess Kikuko on noticing my chilblains. I had never had them before in my life. Like a scolded child I hurriedly hid my hands behind my back.

'You can't help it here,' I explained. 'The wind is so

cold. It's not that I've been doing a lot of washing, or anything!'

They went back to Tokyo after spending the night, but came back again at the end of the month, for another overnight visit, when the two men enjoyed a nice long talk together. Prince Takamatsu was a staff officer on the General Staff, and in a position to know details of the national policy and told Prince Chichibu that war with Britain and America was already inevitable.

The Princess and I were discussing the same thing in another room, feeling that the outlook was gloomy indeed. America and England had deep connections for both myself and the Prince, symbolized in the pattern on the little silver comfit-boxes the Empress Dowager had given us. I was so afraid the news would upset the Prince and worsen his condition.

On 6 December, the newly married Mikasas visited us. It was the first time the Prince had met the bride, and he dressed in his formal *hakama* for the occasion. The following day being Sunday, the young couple spent the night, and after they had gone, the Prince was in a particularly happy mood, full of affectionate reminiscences about his mischievous youngest brother.

Both my husband and Prince Takamatsu were born while Emperor Taishō was still Crown Prince, and being grandchildren of the reigning sovereign, Emperor Meiji, were known as Their Highnesses the Imperial Grandsons, while Prince Mikasa had been born when his father was Emperor, and therefore was a Prince in his own right straight away. His elder brothers used to tease him, saying they were of different birth! It was clear the Prince felt that his little brother, now grown up and married, had become a fine young man with a promising future before him.

The next day after the Mikasas returned to Tokyo – 8 December – Japan declared war on Britain and the United States. That day, a detachment of 12 men from the Sixth Eastern Corps were posted to mount guard at our villa, and we were immediately put on air-raid alert. When he was told the news, the Prince said nothing and only nodded.

It was a war that ignored the nation's resources. Moreover, the Prince had so many good British friends, from the Royal Family down, not to mention teachers. For some while after the start of the war, the Prince hardly spoke at all. He refused to even mention anything to do with the war. When not resting, all he did was sit silently in his study, only gazing for hours at Mount Fuji.

# CHAPTER NINE

# Imperial Villa, Gotemba

---

## FUJI'S FOUR SEASONS

*I*n the old days, it was generally accepted in Japan that women did not discuss politics. They were not supposed to comment or make judgements, and had to refrain from expressing opinions. I trusted the Prince, and believed that all would be well if I only did as he wished. But since the Prince became an invalid, I tried not to trouble him any more than necessary, and therefore had to make decisions and organize some things on my own.

War with America and Britain had just begun. Not only were US Ambassador Joseph Grew and British Ambassador Sir Robert Craigie envoys of countries we had personal connections with, but they and their wives were very good friends of ours. They were about to be repatriated, and we hated to end our friendship in this way. There was no question of being able to meet them and bid them a proper farewell.

It occurred to me that I could ask Shunichi Kase –

who had served under my father, and was now head of the North American section of the American Affairs Bureau of the Foreign Ministry – to see the Grews and the Craigies on our behalf. Together with messages, I entrusted to Mr Kase a jewel-box for Mrs Grew to commemorate our long friendship, and for Lady Craigie some mutton I had managed to obtain in Gotemba and other foodstuffs, since they would be interned for some time yet.

When Mr Kase arrived at the American Embassy, the Grews greeted him in their best clothes, and accepted my message and the jewel-box with tears in their eyes. They were apparently so overcome with emotion it was some time before they could speak. 'We are deeply grateful for such kind treatment by the Imperial Family', said the Ambassador, finally. The Craigies, too, I heard, were delighted, and I believe Sir Robert said to Mr Kase: 'I did not know the details of the negotiations between Japan and America. If only I had known, I could have acted as an intermediary.' As for me, it was a great relief to have been able, thanks to Mr Kase, to let the two Ambassadors and their wives know of the Prince's and my feelings.

About the end of January, 1942, it was decided to build a new annex for the Prince that would be light and airy and get plenty of sunshine, for unless he was forced to rest owing to a slight temperature, he passed the time reading in his study. It was not really a proper building, but more like a makeshift prefab, hurriedly put up with used timber, and had only a plywood *tokonoma* alcove. The main feature was the fact that the whole south side consisted of sliding glass doors, but even the six foot long screen in the bedroom painted by Joyō Nozawa of Hirosaki did little to make the place – with its naked wiring – look less like a warehouse. The Prince felt badly about having new living quarters built for himself in wartime, but I wanted him to get better, and was determined to see that he had the best conditions towards this end.

The Prince moved into his new quarters on 5 April. At this time, besides reading, he used to enjoy working out problems in *shogi* – Japanese chess. He used to say that working out *shogi* problems was not only fun, and a solace, but helped him to keep up his powers of reasoning and made the time pass more quickly.

The Prince was also very fond of *rakugo*, the traditional art of comic story-telling. While convalescing in Gotemba, he frequently listened to it on the radio. This somehow became known, and the leading exponents of the art volunteered to take turns visiting us to entertain the Prince, who used to laugh so hard his glasses kept misting over. Each time he took them off to wipe them, he would turn around to see if I and the staff were laughing too.

When we were trying to find a house in Gotemba I had been insistant that the Prince have a room with a view of Fuji so that he could see the mountain even while lying in bed. He never told me at the time in order to spare my feelings, but it turned out that climbing it once had been quite enough of the mountain for him, and he never wanted to climb it again. But the fact was, that gazing at the mountain from Gotemba, he said he began to see many aspects of Fuji he had never dreamed existed: the way it changed according to the season, and even in the space of a single day, the way its colour and cloud-shapes changed moment by moment. It was a mountain you could never tire of observing. Indeed, he told me, there was something awesome and unapproachable about the way it soared, quietly aloof.

Of all the aspects of Mount Fuji – Fuji in early autumn, Fuji in winter, Fuji in spring – I think the Prince's favourite Fuji was its still snow-capped spring countenance.

The Takamatsus and Mikasas came frequently to visit their elder brother, always staying overnight, and brought news of the outside world to the Prince, who did not listen to the radio or read the papers since he knew how far removed from the truth their reports were. Even when they referred to the Battle of Midway that June – the battle that led to Japan's defeat – the people were not told the true state of affairs. Prince Takamatsu, who was on the General Staff, felt it was essential for Japan to bring the war to a conclusion as soon as posible. Prince Takamatsu, in whom the Prince had every confidence, wrote frequent letters to his brother, as well as telephoning, and made many visits to Gotemba, keeping the Prince well informed regarding the progress of the war. And Prince Mikasa, who visited frequently with the Princess, kept him *au fait* with what the army officers were saying and thinking.

Although the Prince – a reluctant invalid at the foot of Mount Fuji – was forced to be merely an onlooker, he never ceased being anxious about Japan's future, and like the Emperor, was sick at heart.

About the middle of August, a dear friend came to see us – Lieutenant General Masaharu Honma, who although only 55 had been retired from his post as Commander-in-Chief, The Philippines, and sent back to Japan to be put on reserve.

'To think I am actually here visiting Your Highnesses!', said the General, his face lowered to hide his tears and his body shaking with emotion.

Having been the Prince's aide-de-camp, and knowing the Prince so well, he must have known how wretched this secluded life must be for the Prince. And the Prince knowing the circumstances of General Honma's being placed on reserve, could feel for him, too. There was no need for words between them on this memorable reunion. The General had a good grasp of world affairs, and we had heard that the personnel reshuffle was connected with his great anxiety to avoid the fighting on the mainland of Japan, which he knew would inevitably cause temendous loss of life.

When General Honma was at the Philippine front, the Prince had sent him a fan with a painting of Fuji by the great Taikan Yokoyama. 'Indeed, my cup runneth over', said the General. 'Fancy being able to gaze like this at the beauty of the mountain, in the presence of Your Highnesses'. That day, Fuji soared majestically, in all its summer clarity, above the trailing clouds below.

General Honma came several times to visit the Prince, who enjoyed their conversations together so much. But, alas, the further possibility of that pleasure was to end with the end of the war. General Honma entered Sugamo Prison as a war criminal for having been C. in C. in the Philippines, and was taken to Manila in December, 1945, where, charged with being responsible for the Bataan Death March, his life was ended on an execution ground, and he just faded away from this world like dew.

We, who knew so well what a gentle warrior he was, could do nothing to help him. Nothing but bow our heads, silently, toward Mount Fuji, and say a prayer.

We shed tears anew when we learned that in General Honma's diary, an entry in February,1946, addressed to his children, had included the words: 'Your father bows every morning towards the Imperial Palace, and prays for the recovery of Prince Chichibu.' And still, whenever I think of General Honma – and all the

others who died as a result of the war – I am filled with
grief, even today.

At the end of September, 1942, Her Majesty the
Empress Dowager, who was staying at the Numazu
Imperial Villa down on the coast not far away,
honoured us with a visit for the first time since the
Prince had fallen ill. The Prince had been without a
fever for some time, had just had a haircut, and did not
look at all emaciated. He was able to greet his mother
outside the front entrance looking fit and well in his
formal *haori-hakama*.

Because of the contagious nature of the Prince's
illness, it had not been possible for the Emperor and
Empress to visit him, and the Empress Dowager had
also been prevented from visiting him for the same
reason. The mother and son had so much to say to one
another that it was as if a flood-gate had been opened,
and the obvious joy of their meeting brought tears to
my eyes. When it was time for her to leave, I was
almost embarrassed by the profuseness with which Her
Majesty thanked me for nursing and caring for her son.

That day, Fuji looked truly a Sacred Mountain –
soaring in splendid majesty and elegance.

For some time afterwards, the Prince was without
fever, and was able to walk as far as the summer-house.
There, at the spot in the grounds with the best overall
view of Fuji stands a statue of the Prince as
mountaineer. It is by Fumio Asakura, who was Japan's
leading sculptor, and was a wedding present from the
Emperor. The Prince often lingered there, with his
hand resting on the statue. I used to think it was not so
much nostalgia for his mountaineering days, but
nostalgia for his elder brother the Emperor that was
probably in his mind – mixed with sadness for his
inability to be of use to the sovereign, and grief that

they could no longer meet.

Although it was not possible for Their Majesties to visit us themselves, they often sent their chief physician up to Gotemba from the Numazu Villa on their behalf with comforting messages.

Alas, the feverless period did not last long. From the middle of October, the Prince was running a temperature of 37 degrees centigrade.

## ARTIFICIAL PNEUMOTHORAX

From about April 1943, blackouts and firefighting drills had begun – in which I, too, participated – which brought home to us the gravity of the situation.

Although the Prince was running a temperature, I was required to deputize for the Empress on a tour involving three days in Shizuoka Prefecture and three days in Kanagawa Prefecture. Each of the Imperial Princesses were being sent by Her Majesty to visit all the naval hospitals to cheer up the patients. Because of the Prince's illness, I was sent to prefectures nearby, but even then I worried about him and always telephoned as soon as I had reached my lodgings. Previously, the Prince's condition had invariably worsened whenever I was away, but this time it fortunately did not. It was for their country, but oh, how it pained me to see all those sick and wounded servicemen!

On 5 June, there was a state funeral for Admiral Isoroku Yamamoto. The only happy occasion that year that I can recall was the wedding of the Emperor and Empress's eldest daughter Princess Shigeko to Prince Morihiro Higashikuni on 13 October, which I attended. Being wartime, everything was done very simply, but nevertheless the bride looked young and beautiful. It was a nice change to be able to describe to the Prince, on my return, the details of such a joyful occasion and the great happiness of Their Majesties.

The Prince's health seemed to reflect the hopelessness of the military situation, and was worsening. There were no more walks, just complete bed rest. The poems he wrote then are dispirited with the hopelessness of ever being up and about.

> *To be well again,*
> *And to serve my Emperor!*
> *Was my pledge in vain?*
> *For I see no hope ahead*
> *Of ever rising from my bed.*

I could not bring myself to read those poems until after the war, when he was better. He himself wrote about that period:

> When I woke at night, all was quiet, and I could not even hear Setsuko breathing in the next room. There was no sound even from the nurses' room on the other side of the hall. I would suddenly have to cough, and I knew someone would come running if I did, and not wanting to give anyone trouble, I used to bury my head in the quilts and try my utmost to stifle the sound of my coughing.

He was always thinking of others, and trying so hard not to cause anyone any trouble, trying not to disturb our sleep, always maintaining a stiff upper lip so as not to worry us by betraying his despair. If only he had let me share some of that despair!

From 2 January 1944, Dr Denji Terao took over from Army Doctor Junichi Nakamura as a member of the Prince's medical team. Dr Terao was the Health Advisory Chief of the Anti-Tuberculosis Association, as well as being the man who developed the Terao Pneumothorax in 1934. As I explained earlier, when the lung is contracted, the point of entry of the disease is closed off, the discharge of bacilli stopped, and recovery begins. Pneumothorax treatment consists of removing the air from the pleural cavity so that it naturally contracts. It was decided to add this treatment to the general regimen of fresh air, rest, and nourishment he was already following.

Dr Terao describes his first impression of the Gotemba Villa as follows:

> The sick room was a Japanese-style room of eight mats, separated from the corridor partly by a plywood wall, and partly by papered sliding doors behind which was His Highness's bed. . . .The bed faced the veranda on the south side, and on His Highness's right was a *tokonoma*, the sides of which were also plywood. I was astounded at the simplicity. The veranda was of ordinary cypress and only three feet wide. The Princess sat on a blanket spread on the wooden floor. I was amazed at what a plain and humble sick room it was.'

Dr Terao always seemed surprised that I never sat on a cushion, but I had my reasons. In one of his poems, the Prince had written,

> *'The sound of my cough*
> *Changes, and I know that I*
> *Must be getting worse.*
> *How my heart sinks...*

Being unable to take his pain upon me and suffer in his stead, I felt the least I could do was to inflict some discomfort upon myself in sympathy with his condition.

The Prince was no longer able to walk to his study, but spent all day in bed. In the morning he mainly read – books on law, art and literature. He rested in the afternoon, much of the time gazing at Mount Fuji. In the evening, he would often listen to the radio. His days were invariably spent like this until the war ended.

On 19 May the Prince suffered a severe spontaneous pneumothorax attack and nearly died of asphyxiation. Dr Terao, in the presence of several consultants including Dr Ryūkichi Inada, the then foremost authority on tuberculosis, inserted a hypodermic needle and extracted the air that had invaded the pleural cavity through burst tissue, and saw the Prince through the crisis. To insert a needle into a royal chest was indeed a very bold step at that time, when princes and princesses might not even be vaccinated arbitrarily.

Six days after the emergency, the Prince's condition had more or less stabilized, except that water formed in the lungs, and had to be removed and replaced by air. Once more, artificial pneumothorax was indicated. Up until then, the thickened pleura of the Prince's left lung had prevented the details of his lung from being visible in X-rays, and it was assumed that adhesion would make pneumothorax impossible. But a spontaneous pneumothorax having occurred, the lung, as well as rupturing, had effectively contracted. Now, the bacilli in the Prince's sputum were diminishing daily.

On 22 July 1944, the Tōjō cabinet withdrew, and General Kuniaki Koiso became Prime Minister. From mid-October, the Prince was able to get up, and only needed artificial pneumothorax occasionally.

By November, air-raid warnings could be heard daily, as B29s flew past in formation over the Villa. Saipan having surrendered, air raids on the Japanese mainland had become a possibility. Gotemba was on the flight path of the B29s as they made for Tokyo. They would come in over Suruga Bay, and fly over

Mount Fuji and Hakone, and each time they passed overhead, we would instinctively fold our hands together and pray that casualties would be light. But each day the damage got worse and worse. Trains stopped so often that finally Dr Endo, the Prince's head physician, moved to Gotemba.

In December, although the Prince donated over 223 trees from our cypress forest to the war effort, he would not allow us to obtain the necessary flour from the black market to mix with taro yams and ginger for his chest poultices. I would have gladly gone without food, clothing and shelter for his sake, and not to be able to get this necessity for him depressed me.

But by now, the Prince's condition did not seem too bad, and the chief physician's cheerful countenance made me happier than anything.

However, the air raids continued without respite, and on 25 February 1945, fire bombs fell on the Imperial Palace in Tokyo, and part of the Emperor's residence and that of the Empress Dowager were burned. I paid a visit to Their Majesties on 6 March to enquire as to their welfare, and was happy to be able to assure those at home on my return that no one had been injured. What a relief it had been to find that the Empress Dowager was safe, and that the only damage she had sustained had been to the three-story tower of her palace, and the glass doors and sliding paper partitions. I hurried back to Gotemba to the wail of sirens.

But no sooner had I returned to Gotemba than there was an enormous air raid on Tokyo lasting from midnight on 9 March to the 10th, in which we heard that the official residence of the Imperial Household Minister had burned down. Fortunately, both my father and mother were safe. Ever since my father had been appointed to that post, realizing the gravity of his responsibilities, they had vacated the house in Shōto, and moved completely into the official residence. Being a single-minded man, devoted to duty, my father did not even consider evacuation, and therefore lost everything.

'So now I'm just an ordinary person, like everybody else', he said.

In January, 1941, he had lost, to an illness, his darling youngest son Jiro, the apple of his eye, not yet quite seventeen, whom we used to call 'Ji' for short. After that, material loss meant little to him.

## 15 AUGUST 1945

Iwo-jima had fallen on 17 March. And as if that was not enough, still they came, night and day – the B29s in formations a hundred, and two hundred strong. It broke our hearts to think of the havoc they would be wreaking far and wide.

As for the Prince's fight against his illness, there was not much cause for optimism although the crisis was over for the time being. Dr Endō and Dr Terao were kept busy administering the difficult artificial pneumothorax treatment and the drawing out of fluid from the chest.

Because of the daily air raids, visits by members of the Imperial Family became less frequent, although the Mikasas did manage to come in between raids. Prince Takamatsu was too busy with the pressure of work at Staff Headquarters to leave Tokyo, but wrote weekly.

On 7 April, the Kantarō Suzuki cabinet was formed. A month later, on 7 May, Germany surrendered unconditionally, and although Japan's defeat seemed certain to us, the militarists were all for making a stand on the homeland. Camouflage was applied to our roof, and a strong air raid shelter was made for us by soldiers from the Tōkai Corps. It was dug in a spiral, like a snail's shell, with an escape shaft at the very end, and if necessary, the Prince would be carried to the inner-most recess on a stretcher. There was also a simpler shelter built by the Imperial Household.

Meanwhile, I worked hard growing vegetables. Even if we did not become self-sufficient, it helped to have something extra. But never having grown anything but roses, I found hoeing and tilling hard work indeed. Masako Shirasu's husband made us an oven for baking bread, and we managed to make some tasty loaves out of a variety of grains and cereals.

About that time, Tokyo suffered another devastating air raid. It was on 25 May, and this time both the Emperor's Palace and that of the Empress Dowager were burned. Our residence, too, in Omote-machi, was reduced to ashes – except for part of the Japanese section – and two guards lost their lives. The Prince's Private Secretary came to see us, to apologize profoundly for having been unable to save the Prince's many prized books, among which were valuable foreign books and specialized volumes.

'Seven of us,' he said, 'did our utmost to save the books, but, alas, they all burned to a crisp.'

What could seven men – or more – with buckets, hope to do against a bombing raid by over two hundred B29s!

The Prince thanked him and urged him not to worry about it any more. 'It was something entirely beyond your control', he said.

Even after dealing such a fatal blow to Tokyo, the B29s did not stop their bombing. The Emperor and Empress moved into a residence which had escaped the fire. The Emperor's personal office was set up there too. I was finally able to get to Tokyo on 27 May, but instead of replying to my enquiries about the Palace fire, the Empress kept asking me about the Prince's health and thanking me for braving the air raids to come to see them, all she would speak about was her anxiety for all the people who had lost their homes and their loved ones.

The Ninomaru Gardens in the palace grounds, once so lovely with azaleas and irises, were a desolate ruin, and I missed the usual sound of murmuring water in the Fukiage Gardens in the north-western part of the estate. The once limpid stream, where fireflies used to flit about on summer evenings, seemed to be silently choking back its tears with sadness.

I met the Empress Dowager in her air-raid shelter. She, too, would not talk about the burning of her palace, but only spoke about the ordeal of the Japanese people.

'Take good care of Yasuhito', she said as I took leave of her, after assuring Her Majesty that her son's health was beginning to look a little better.

Lastly, I visited our Tokyo home. I was prepared for the worst, but the ruins looked even more pitiful than I had imagined. I had been instructed by the Prince not to refer to anything that was burned, but only to thank people and give them encouragement. He told me to find out the names of those guards who had lost their lives and arrange for someone to represent us at their funerals. In the midst of so much that was changed beyond recognition, it was comforting to find the age-old deodars and other trees still standing, albeit with their leaves somewhat singed.

On 4 June, my father, after apologizing personally to the Emperor, resigned his post as Imperial Household

Minister to take responsibility for the Palace's destruction by fire. Soon after the end of the war, he sold his property in Shibuya Ward's Shōto district and moved to Senzoku. Even though not all of his property had been destroyed in the air raids and subsequent fires, the Emperor's Palace was gone, and His Majesty inconvenienced. My father felt it would not be proper to live to the same standard as before. I heard later that he let the Government of Tokyo have our old property at a price far below its value, which was so like my father, and it is now the official residence of the Governor.

By the 26th, the Prince was well enough to take walks in the grounds of our Villa, but Dr Endō and Dr Terao continued their medical supervision. Artificial pneumothorax had been suspended from the beginning of June, but there was no telling when it might become necessary again. Meanwhile, I worked in the vegetable garden every day, in my straw hat and *monpe* dungarees, ignoring the air-raid warnings.

On the 30th, no sooner had the air-raid siren gone than there were some very loud booms in the direction of Gotemba Station, only three kilometres to our east. It was obviously bombs. My helpers and I ran back to the house, and with all of us gathered around the Prince, we took refuge in the shelter for the first time. We later heard that several carrier-based aircraft had strafed the area around the railway station and dropped eight 50-kilogram bombs.

The Prince had begun thinking ever since July that the constant bombing by the American forces must be in preparation for some special assault. His assumption was unfortunately correct. On 6 August the atom bomb was dropped on Hiroshima, followed by the one on Nagasaki on the 9th. Moreover, the USSR had entered the war against Japan, and earlier, on 21 June, Okinawa had fallen. An American attack on Japan's mainland would be next, and while the Japanese Army expected a swift attack by the Americans, by this time, I think most of the Japanese people had lost their will to fight.

From Prince Takamatsu's letters and his ADC's reports, I think the Prince was pretty much aware of how the war had changed, and how its end was taking shape.

On 15 August, at the very height of the summer heat, Prince and Princess Takamatsu arrived by car from Tokyo at about 11.30 in the morning. On looking back, I think the reason they came here, leaving Tokyo so early in the morning, was because Prince Takamatsu wanted to be with his brother, and could not bear the thought of listening without him to the important, historic, unprecedented broadcast by the Emperor to the people. Or it may have simply been that he felt his bedridden brother needed his support at this time.

The Prince sat up in bed, and we all gathered around him there to listen to the noon broadcast on his bedside radio. There was a lot of static, probably because of the mountains round about Gotemba, so we could not hear His Majesty's voice very clearly. But I remember my eyes filling with tears, both with relief that the war was over, and the multitude of thoughts that welled up in my mind. I cannot remember what the brothers said after the broadcast, or what the general feeling was. The Takamatsus had said they would have to return to Tokyo at once, so all I could think of was what to give them for lunch before they left.

That day, the Prince had to have a pneumothorax treatment and lung fluid extraction for the first time in three months. He was bound to have been affected by this great turning point in history.

But he felt fine the very next day. Prince Mikasa arrived, and spent the night with us, and in spite of the Prince's invalid condition, it transpired that we would have to leave immediately for Tokyo. I went first on the 19th to make arrangements, and the Prince followed two days later.

CHAPTER TEN

# *The Post-war Years*

THE SHMOO

*T*he reason we had to leave Gotemba so suddenly was that the GHQ of the American armed forces' occupation, to be centred on Yokohama, had issued an order that Japanese army personnel, and anyone else connected with the army, must get out of an area that included the northern part of Shizuoka Prefecture. The Higashikuni cabinet, formed on the 17th, had sent us a message saying that since Gotemba was on the edge of the area, we should move to Tokyo if at all possible. Both doctors felt it was risky, but we left Gotemba at 1 p.m., with Dr Endō and I accompanying the Prince in his car, stopping on the way for a brief rest at Marquis Nabeshima's seaside villa in Oiso.

After a hot, tiring ride, it was a great relief when we finally arrived in Tokyo without the Prince having suffered any ill effects from the drive. All that was left of our old Akasaka residence was four tatami-matted rooms of the Japanese section. The Prince had hardly ever set foot in them before, but now they represented a roof over our heads, for which we were thankful. The rooms were not elegant, and quite draughty, but that was a blessing in the humid summer weather. There was no kitchen, but Princess Takamatsu had kindly provided us with a sink and a refrigerator, which we gratefully installed in a corner of the veranda. A few chairs in one of the rooms had to suffice for the Prince to receive the Prime Minister, Prince Higashikuni, Foreign Minister Yoshida, and others who came to pay their respects. Prince Takamatsu came every day, but usually just sat informally on the edge of the veranda without coming in.

The Prince got though the end of the summer heat without incident, and began to feel well enough to walk all around the burnt-out estate. On the afternoon of 15 September, I accompanied him to the Palace. His first meeting with his brother the Emperor since falling ill five years before was a deeply emotional reunion. For the last time, the Prince wore the uniform of a major-general – but without his sword, now that the war was over. The Emperor seemed delighted to see his brother looking so well, and they had so much to say to one another it was half past five before we left.

By October, I began to be worry about the effect our draughty temporary abode night have on the Prince's health as winter approached. The doctors were worried, too, and we were given permission by the Americans to move back to Gotemba on 1 November. Fuji was resplendent in early snow, the plants in the vegetable garden had been well-tended in our absence and had grown apace, and we were happy to be back. Although it was only little over a month since we had left, wondering if we would ever return, so much had happened in that short time that it seemed as if we had been away for ages. We had been an occupied country since 30 August when General MacArthur, Supreme Commander Allied Powers, landed at the former Naval Air Station at Atsugi. Everything had changed radically and bewilderingly. Only Mount Fuji remained the same, soaring aloof – nobody's captive. Rather than living a gloomy and servile life as people of an occupied country, I hoped we could just obey the Army of Occupation's rules and go forward in friend-ship, shoulder to shoulder with them.

The Prince was an optimist; a practical man with a positive outlook. While we were living in the remains of our burned-out Tokyo residence, a friend of mine from Hiroshima came to call while I was out. Her husband, the Vice-Governor, had been killed by the atom bomb, while she and her five children were saved by taking refuge in the river. She had come to thank me for the clothes and other things I had sent her. She told me the Prince said to her: 'Don't worry. You'll see. Japan will make a fine recovery. So make sure you bring up your children well. The war is over. The Japanese people are going to work hard. We're not the sort of nation and not the sort of people to go to pieces. There is nothing to worry about. Everything is going to be all right. Japan will most certainly rise again.'

My friend took the Prince's words to heart, and today her children are indeed fine members of society.

Food shortages had been severe for some time, so we dug up the gardens and the tennis court to grow more food. We tried hard to prepare nutritious meals for the Prince, but he had always been a simple 'soup and two-vegetables' man for preference, and would screw up his face if presented with anything too fancy.

One day, an American journalist came to interview the Prince. 'Your Highness, is there anything you need, or anything you would like?' he asked. To which the Prince replied, purposely looking serious: 'Yes, there is something I want badly. I have been taking the Occupation newspaper and reading it every day, and in it I've been reading a comic strip in which there is something called a "Shmoo". Apparently, if one has a shmoo, one can make anything one wants. I would very much like to have a shmoo. If the Japanese had some shmoos, I'm sure they would be able to reconstruct their country and everything would be all right!'

'Wow! So Your Highness knows about shmoos!'

The journalist was delighted, and sent us the biggest shmoo you ever saw. It was folded flat and when the parcel arrived we wondered what on earth it could be. When we blew it up it was enormous. The Prince was thrilled with his shmoo, and even had his picture taken with it. The photograph appeared in the Occupation newspaper, and people sent us lots and lots of shmoos.

'This is all we need for Japan's recovery', the Prince used to say.

In those days the general public still had ambivalent feelings towards the Occupation and found it hard to get used to. I am quite certain the Prince's sense of humour and delight evidenced in the shmoo episode was the very first step in post World-War II Japan-American goodwill and friendship.

THE PRINCE CHICHIBU FARM

The Prince's post-war dream was to live an English-style country life, farming on a large enough scale to be completely self-sufficient as to food. We put some acreage under cultivation and grew not just kitchen-garden vegetables, as we had during the war, but crops

such as potatoes, sweet potatoes, buckwheat, pump-
kins, sweet corn, and finally even wheat and upland
rice. Besides chickens, we kept sheep and goats. At one
time we kept pigs, and later even raised milking cows.
We even produced a small amount of sweet potatoes
and wheat for the market, stressing quality rather than
quantity. But when all was said and done, it was an
amateur operation, and many were the funny happen-
ings and episodes.

The Prince undertook some of the light work at first,
such as weeding, picking off insects, treading wheat,
and herding sheep, but as he regained his health, he
took on harvesting wheat and making compost, as well
as the arduous task in summer under the scorching sun
of cutting grass to make winter hay to feed the cows
and goats.

At first my ladies-in-waiting and I were quite hopeless
at hoeing, so the Prince asked a teacher from the
Gotemba agricultural college to come and give us
lessons. Oh, how difficult we found it to learn the
knack of how to wield a hoe and dig a straight furrow!
We tried so hard, dressed in our peasant overalls, with
the sweat running down our faces, but we hardly ever
got our rows straight the first time and would invariably
be made to do them over again. We certainly acquired a
great respect for the work of farmers.

In his eagerness for us all to experience fully the life
of the English landed gentry, which he had observed
first-hand while in England, the Prince got experts to
come from the prefectural breeding centre to teach us
how to milk our sheep and goats. The Prince loved
being able to drink the fresh milk and offer it to our
guests, who found our home-grown potatoes and corn
a treat as well. There is nothing like freshly-picked
corn. If not eaten within four hours of harvesting, corn-

on-the-cob begins to dry out and the flavour deterio-rates. The Prince always sent any particularly good produce of ours first to the Empress Dowager, whose obvious delight used to encourage him greatly.

The Takamatsus and the Mikasas visited us fre-quently, and enjoyed the freedom of life in Gotemba and the informal family gatherings impossible in Tokyo. In those desperately food-scarce post-war times, we had plenty of fresh chicken, eggs, and milk, in addition to what was provided by generous American relief agencies.

Keeping full-grown pigs had turned out not to be feasible because of our shortage of feed, so the Prince gave all our pigs away to neighbouring farms with the proviso that they give us back one piglet from each litter, which we would then raise and return when it was grown. The Prince thought up this scheme to help the farms to prosper, but alas, it did not work. In those days few farmers had the time and means to do much more than just exist from day to day. It transpired that after they received their pigs they immediately sold them! Raising pigs should have been a profitable enterpprise. In reality, it was not a success. The Prince's Private Secretary, who was in charge of transferring the pigs, was upset. 'You can't very well tell them not to sell the pigs...' he used to mutter. It was quite funny, really, but rather sad at the same time.

The Prince began to be more and more ambitious in his role as English-style gentleman farmer, and put in electrically-heated beds for sprouting seeds and machines for threshing and milling, which he allowed local farmers to use. The Prince tried out tractors, as well as experimenting in various other ways. It was all rather hit or miss, and he had some real failures, learning much about the harshness of nature in the process. But the joy of a good harvest gave all of us tremendous fulfilment.

The Prince and I took lessons in spinning and weaving, and we made homespun from the wool of our sheep. We became known by our neighbours as The Prince's Experimental Farm, and the fact that it brought us into such close and friendly contact with the local people was one of the nicest results of our agricultural project.

Above all, the Prince wanted our household to be one big happy family. He loved to organize competitions. 'Fuji Prosperity', the name of the brown draught ox, was chosen this way. He also had everyone compete in making bird feeders of their own design to place wherever they wanted in the grounds, and gave a prize to the person whose feeder attracted the most birds. The Prince loved to invent things, and one of his designs was a vegetable dehydrator he set under the floor of the house.

During this time, I often made trips to Tokyo on the Prince's behalf. Following General MacArthur's Occupation Policy a directive was issued abolishing privilege regarding Imperial Family property, and so we had to fill out a tax return like ordinary citizens, which I then took to the Imperial Household Agency. I also represented the Prince at an Imperial Family conference when the new Constitution came into force on 3 May 1947. Its revised Imperial Family code decreed that besides the Emperor's sons, only three princes would be allowed to retain their Imperial status – his brothers Prince Chichibu, Prince Takamatsu and Prince Mikasa.

We had had to give up our Hayama villa of so many memories in April, 1946, after one last winter there.

On 18 October 1947, both the Prince and I went to a

farewell dinner at the Akasaka Detached Palace, attended by their Majesties the Emperor and Empress and the Empress Dowager, for the former members of the Imperial Family whose Imperial status had been abolished.

'Let us always keep in touch', said the Emperor, raising his glass, and when, in reply, the now former Prince Morimasa Nashimoto raised his, saying, 'I pray for the continued prosperity of the Imperial Family,' I was choked with emotion, and at the same time, suddenly aware of the weight of responsibility now resting upon those few of us who officially remained Imperial.

'I ENVY THE WEEDS'

'No matter how often you keep pulling them up, weeds just keep on growing', observed my old childhood friend Masako Kabayama Shirasu.

'I envy the weeds', said the Prince, as if to himself.

Something about the way he said it alarmed me. It made me realize how frail he was in spite of his seemingly restored health since the end of the war. He was working much too hard, and not eating properly. We would try and make meals more nourishing by doing things like mixing egg into his corn dumplings, in spite of his objection to such surreptitious measures. In 1949 his fever began to rise again, necessitating a kidney operation. He made good progress, and when the Emperor and Empress visited us during his convalescence, he proudly showed them round the farm. The Empress Dowager, visited frequently, whenever she was staying at the nearby Numazu Villa, and mother and son had many happy informal talks together. She promised soon to pay us a longer visit of several days, so she could listen to the birds singing.

We had told her how at dawn around 4 a.m., first there is the *canna-canna-canna* of the evening cicada, and then the hoot of an owl, followed by the songs of a paradise flycatcher, Siberian meadow bunting, and great tit, before the cock begins to crow in the poultry house. And then you hear the cuckoo, the brown-eared bulbul, and the screech of the azure-winged magpie. During his long illness, the Prince waking early, learned to know the various songs and the time of day that each bird sang. Alas, I managed to learn only a few. How I regret not having got the Prince to teach me how to identify more of them.

In 1950, two chest operations were performed, from which the Prince made a fairly good recovery thanks to the streptomycin sent by the Royal Family of Norway and also that made available by the Americans. It did not cure the tuberculosis, but undoubtedly prolonged the Prince's life and enabled him to take part in a variety of local events. But no more farm work.

Not being able to participate any longer in sports or public duties, the Prince had taken up writing, and contributed a series of essays in 1948 entitled 'Diary of a Convalescent' to a health magazine, hoping it would help to encourage TB sufferers. The Prince had already published a book entitled 'Recollections of life in England and America' (to which I contributed the American section ), as well as a book entitled 'Gotemba Thoughts'.

Sometime during that summer, the Prince began to complain of pains in his left chest. Diagnosed as caries of the rib cartilege, immediate surgery was indicated. A two-hour operation was carried out on August 12th, from which his recovery was, thankfully, swift.

One of the Prince's hobbies at this time was pottery making. He had a kiln installed, and after taking lessons, and when his state of health allowed, greatly enjoyed turning pots and tea bowls, which he dubbed 'Mitsumine ware' after his beloved Three Peaks in the Chichibu Mountains.

Now that there were only three princely houses left, I had often to represent the Prince in Tokyo on some official duty or other, as well as taking his place at Japan-British Society functions and sports events. And then there was the Tuberculosis Prevention Association of which I was the honorary President. All this kept me away frequently.

When the Prince was with me, naturally we went by car, but when I went alone, I always took the train. Together with my senior lady-in-waiting, Kuni Kawazu, we rode on the local Gotemba line, changing to the main Tōkaidō line, and always travelled second class, both during the war and after. I saw a lot, learned a lot, and experienced much kindness. I became so used to riding on the Gotemba line I called it 'my train', and almost everyone who rode it knew me by sight. I was reminded the other day of the time I kept the flies away from a nursing mother. It was during the war, and the train, as usual, was full of foragers, travelling into the country hoping to find food. It was different on the Tōkaidō line, especially during the rush hour, so we made a point of wearing our *monpe* farm overalls, so as not to be conspicuous. We changed into other clothes when we reached our destination. So many things amazed me as I rode on trains, making me realise how out of touch with reality we Imperials were.

It was raining on 17 May 1951, when news reached us for which we were totally unprepared. The Empress Dowager had died of a sudden heart attack. The Prince was not well enough to travel, but I hurried to Tokyo. It was hard to believe that her promise to spend several days with us would now never materialize. We had looked forward to it so eagerly, and had only that day ordered the tatami renewed for her visit. I felt as if my main prop and stay had been pulled out from under me. As for the Prince, who had had such a specially close relationship with his mother, he was overwhelmed with grief that he of all people, was unable to be at her wake. To support him in his grief, I resolved to allow myself no tears.

He insisted on attending the the ceremony on the 19th of the placing of the body in the coffin. I went back to Gotemba to accompany him up to Tokyo in the car, together with two doctors, for the long drive. Although he rested for several hours, he looked very tired when the 7 p.m. ceremony was over.

We stayed in Tokyo until after the Ceremony of the Fortieth Day so the Prince could attend many of the rites, including the Proclamation of the Posthumous Name: Empress Teimei. While in town the Prince underwent a great many medical examinations. It was 28 June before we returned to Gotemba. I went back to Tokyo alone for the final 50th Day Rite, and that night I let myself go and had my first really good cry at the loss of my beloved mentor, guide and friend.

> *In my grief, my tears*
> *Flow on and on, when I think*
> *How Your Majesty*
> *Was the one who tutored me,*
> *And made me what I am today.*

THE OXFORD RUGBY TEAM

At the beginning of September, a whiteness would

appear each morning on the summit of Fuji. The Prince would have the whole household assembled and ask us each to guess whether it was frost or snow. After everyone had given the mountain a good stare with naked eyes, the Prince would take a look with his binoculars and determine which it was. Those who guessed correctly were rewarded with a sweet or a piece of cake.

It was fun, but we dreaded the cold winter our game presaged. Gotemba was a summer resort, and winters there were severe. When electricity restrictions were in force, the Prince would not let us apply for special permission to use electric heaters. The only alternative was a potbellied stove, which would not be good for his lungs. Eventually, a suitable house for the winter was found on a quiet south-facing hill in Kugenuma, a seaside resort near Fujisawa. The upstairs rooms were sunny, the garden large enough to put in a few of the Prince's favourite plants, and it was also within easy reach of Tokyo.

We moved there in January, 1952. The Prince liked the house, which was a great relief to me, but I worried for fear the constant stream of visitors, engendered by its accessibility, would tire him. But surprisingly, he thrived so well that his team of four doctors only needed to attend about once a month. The mild climate of Kugenuma seemed to agree with the Prince. In April, we had shrubs such as red and white blossoming plum, hawthorn, kerria, laurel, and juniper brought from the ruins of our Tokyo property, and the Prince supervized their replanting. He also received a mimosa and two coconut palms from his old school friend the former Viscount Hachisuka.

Having attended his coronation, the news of King George VI's death on 6 February saddened us greatly, and our hearts went out in special sympathy to the widowed Queen, of whom we had such fond memories.

The Peace Treaty, signed on 28 April, made Japan an independent country once more, which meant that someone from Japan would be invited to the coronation of Queen Elizabeth II the following year. The Prince felt strongly that it would be in the best interest of both Japan and the Crown Prince for the latter to represent the Emperor. The Anglo-Japanese political climate not being what it had been before, he felt it absolutely essential that the Crown Prince should go, and pressed the matter fervently with Imperial Household Agency Chief Tajima and Dr Shinzō Koizumi.

In a letter to the Household Agency Chief, the Prince set down his reasons as follows. 1) The Crown Prince was of the same generation as the Queen and for him to make her acquaintance now would be of benefit to the future of both nations. 2) Although the Crown Prince had only recently come of age and many people feared he lacked sufficient experience, he would only be one of many guests, and therefore could be fairly relaxed. 3) From his own experience of attending the coronation of George VI, he knew that most monarchies would be represented by a crown prince, and other countries by top-ranking people, and so he believed that it would be of great significance for him to take advantage of this matchless opportunity to meet all those people at one time. And 4), while the British had mixed feelings towards Japan, the Crown Prince was still a boy and clearly had no connection with the war, so it was very important for the future that friendly relations with other countries be forged anew, and he was the ideal one to represent the Emperor compared with the other members of the Imperial Family, who all served in the armed forces.

I am quite sure this advice from the Prince was crucial to the decision made by Imperial Household Agency Chief Tajima.

The Oxford University Rugby Team came to Japan in September, and we spent a fortnight in Tokyo so that the Prince could attend the team's matches against Japanese universities. He hosted a party for the Oxford team to which he also invited Crown Prince Akihito, and was delighted to see the latter chatting with the Oxford men. The Prince was anxious for the Crown Prince's sake that there should be at least a few people with feelings of goodwill towards Japan while he was a guest at Queen Elizabeth's coronation in Britain, where anti-Japanese sentiments still remained.

We returned to Gotemba once, but soon came back to Tokyo to attend the Investiture of the Crown Prince. After the Ceremony on November 10th, we remained in Tokyo, and the Prince managed to maintain a full schedule in Tokyo for several days at a time, receiving ambassadors in audience, and attending embassy parties, all to make sure that the Crown Prince met and conversed with the ambassadors and dignitaries of as many countries as possible.

When the Crown Prince left for England the following year, in June, 1953, the British Government issued a statement that he would receive an official welcome, and a reception was held in his honour. But by then, alas, Prince Chichibu had already departed this life.

Neither did he live to see the completion that same year of the Prince Chichibu Rugby Stadium, which commemorates for posterity his love for the game and his services to it in Japan. How it delights me to see it steadily gaining in popularity here. I have been told it is the only sports arena in this country named after a specific person. In the post-war years, while baseball stadiums proliferated and fans of the game increased rapidly, rugby lagged behind because although there were people who wanted to play it and promote it, there was no suitable ground. So a group of enthusiasts got together and made a rugby field themselves, with their own bare hands, in part of the outer gardens of the Meiji Shrine. When he heard about it, the Prince, in spite of his illness, made a point of visiting the work-site every time he was in Tokyo.

After seeing his first rugby match during his student days in England, the Prince never missed a match if he could help it, either there or in Japan. I shall never forget the first time I accompanied him to one. It was while we were in Kyoto for Emperor Shōwa's Enthronement, and took place at a prestigious high school so soon after the Ceremony that I did not have time to wash the heavy camellia grease out of my hair. It was all I could do to change out my heavy ceremonial twelve-layered robe of ancient design into Western dress. My hair had to stay as it was, hidden by a scarf!

When the Oxford University Rugby Team played against Keio University in Tokyo, in September, 1952, I was told how the Prince insisted on going all the way down to the field to greet each of the players personally, and how tremendously exhausted he was after climbing the many stairs back up to the royal box. It was evident to me then how deep was his nostalgia for the Oxford of his interrupted studies to which he was never able to return, and his love for the game of rugby.

LAST WILL AND TESTAMENT

The Prince died at Kugenuma in the early dawn of 4 January 1953. His last will and testament, written in a notebook, reads as follows:

> 'Looking back on the fifty years of my life, I feel nothing but gratefulness. I can only say that the life has ended of a very, very ordinary human being who just happened to be born into a position of special privilege with unlimited benefits.
>
> I was indeed far too favoured during my last ten years, spending a quiet life of convalescence while countless people suffering from the same disease as I died in unspeakable privation at a time in history when my people and my country were caught between unprecedented difficult times and hardship. Therefore, not having been able to do anything for my people, nor anything for humanity at large, so I would like at least to be of a little use to mankind at the end of my life. If Setsuko is not against it – I mean rather if she can stomach it – I would like my body to undergo an autopsy.'

He goes on to name the parts to be dissected and examined and the doctors that he wished to have witness it, including 'others specializing in tuberculosis' and finally adding, 'subject to Setsuko's consent'. He further asks that the body be cremated, that there be no tomb, and that the final rite be very simple, 'since it only concerns Setsuko and me'. And if possible, I wish there to be no religious ceremony of any denomination.

Having obtained His Majesty's consent, an autopsy was performed on the night of 5 January. Since whatever the Prince wished would be my wish too, I raised no objections. The funeral, which took place on a rainy January 12th in the garden of the Toshimagaoka mausoleum, was basically in the Imperial Shinto tradition, but in accordance with the wishes stated in the Prince's will, was performed by those who had been closest to him. His former private secretary, Toshio Maeda, acted as chief priest, assisted by the Prince's classmate Sadao Yamaguchi, who had been his *aide-de-camp*. The pallbearers were representatives of various sports from the Japan Athletic Association, and musicians from the the Imperial Household Music Department performed pieces such as Beethoven's '*Les adieux* and Tchaikovsky's *Andante Cantabile*. Afterwards, his body was cremated – the first time ever for a member of the Imperial Family – and his ashes were buried in a graveyard in a corner of the mausoleum. It was all very unconventional, but I think it was more or less what the Prince would have wanted, and was made possible by the Emperor's warm understanding and Prince Takamatsu's help.

> *How you must have loved*
> *Your princely elder brother,*
> *To have helped so much!*
> *How your kindness solaced me,*
> *Dear Prince of Takamatsu!*

For the Fortieth Day Observance on 12 February, the Emperor and Empress came over from Hayama to our villa in Kugenuma. Barely a year before, the Prince had supervized the replanting there of some of his favourite plants from our Tokyo property. Among them was a red and white plum in fragrant blossom. The Emperor sighed with deep emotion as he contemplated it, and later sent me this poem:

> *The potted plum-tree:*
> *How fresh its fragrance fills the air!*
> *Even though, alas,*

> *My brother is no longer there*
> *To enjoy its purity.*

When the Fiftieth Day Observance was over, visitors paying condolence calls tapered off, and I was alone most of the time, just thinking about the Prince and missing him so. There were times when I wondered if there was not some way to join him without causing too much trouble for those around me. During those times, writing poetry was a consolation.

> *The Empress Mother*
> *Is gone, and so are you, my Prince;*
> *What am I to do?*
> *Who am I to lean upon,*
> *How can I go on alone?*

> *Why so soon, my love,*
> *Did you have to leave this world,*
> *When so many here*
> *Loved you so, and needed you,*
> *And were loth to let you go?*

In spite of the cold winter rain, over fifty thousand people from the general populace thronged the road outside the mausoleum at the time of the Prince's funeral, and I noticed a great many of them wiping tears from their eyes. They included students, young people, old people, farmers, housewives, office-workers, and former soldiers. Most of them were people who had only known the Prince through the newspapers and magazines, but loved and admired him. To them he was the 'Sports Prince' and the 'Mountaineering Prince.'

My mother was a tower of strength and scarcely left my side in the days after my bereavement, when I needed her most. She died in 1969, after a long illness.

> *Many were the times*

*I might have gone to pieces,*
  *In my heart's despair*
*Had I not been supported*
*By my mother's tender care.*

*Even when apart,*
  *As, perforce, most times we were,*
    *Knowing she was there*
*Was my only underprop*
*And my comfort and my stay.*

Just a year before, the Prince had moved a deep-red
plum tree to Kugenuma from the Empress Dowager's
Palace as a memento of his late mother. This red plum,
blossoming later than the red-and-white variety, burst
into bloom at the end of February, making me sad all
over again.

*As the evening falls,*
  *I wonder in what garden*
    *They are chatting now:*
*My beloved Prince and Her*
*Late Majesty, his mother.*

As spring progressed, the trees putting forth new
shoots, the flowers, the azure-winged magpie that came
to our window at breakfast, for whom we used to put
out bread-crumbs – everything reminded me of the
Prince.

*Seeing Mount Fuji,*
  *Always reminds me of you,*
    *Beside the window;*
*And birdsong, too,*
*Always reminds me of you.*

*Of my memories,*
  *None are happier than those*
    *Of mountains and of seas*

*We visited together,*
*And foreign lands you took me to.*

*I will bear with pride*
    *Thy name and reputation*
        *And hold them high,*
*So all may remember thee*
*Through me, until the day I die.*

*Although my tears*
    *Will never bring you back to me,*
        *As well I know,*
*At night, when I'm all alone,*
*Tears well up, and flow, and flow.*

# CHAPTER ELEVEN

# *International Friendship*

## THE LITTLE HOUSE

*T*he Prince had been gone a year when I returned to Tokyo to live in the small part of our house that had escaped the fire-bombing. During the 17 or 18 years I lived there I enjoyed many happy contacts with people from other lands. One of the happiest events I experienced while there was the marriage of the present Emperor, when Crown Prince, to Michiko Shōda.

Speaking of Crown Prince Akihito, I remember meeting Mrs Vining, who had come to teach him English. Coming from America, where there was no royal family, she sought advice from my mother on Japanese court etiquette, and they became good friends. She was a lovely lady, elegant and refined, wise and intelligent.

My mother also advised Princess Michiko on court etiquette before her wedding. I think the Empress, as she is now, must have fond memories of my mother from those days, because every May 8th, the anniversary of my mother's death, she sends me flowers from her garden. Freshly picked, the flowers are sometimes wrapped in beautiful handmade *washi* paper, and sometimes artistically arranged in baskets. I apppreciate Her Majesty's thoughtful kindness, and am sure my mother does too.

In November, 1961, when Princess Alexandra came to Japan on an official mission to present the Emperor with a letter of goodwill greetings from the Queen, I was chosen to officially welcome Her Royal Highness because of Prince Chichibu's close connection with Britain, having studied at Oxford University and been the Honorary Patron of the Japan-British Society, which position I now held. Afterwards, she wanted to see a social welfare organization, so I accompanied her to see some of the activities of the Japan Red Cross. She was extremely interested in everything, and although we only had a few minutes to spare, I brought her home, to see how I lived. She was immensely intrigued by my *hori-gotatsu*, the heated sunken pit in the tatami floor under the low table. She immediately tried it out, and seemed to find the idea delightful. 'You can sit here and do all sorts of things,' she said, looking as if she would have liked to stay longer. She had only just been born when I met her parents, the Duke and Duchess of Kent, at the Coronation of her uncle King George VI.

While British royal children were usually taught at home, Princess Alexandra went to an ordinary school, and then studied nursing in a hospital. Princess Alexandra was the first member of the British Royal Family to visit Japan since the Duke of Gloucester came 32 years earlier, and I could not help but think what a perfect goodwill ambassador she was for Queen Elizabeth's new reign.

It was Prince Charles who called my post-war Tokyo home 'The Little House'. Approaching it from across the garden of the Crown Prince's palace, it did look tiny. All the members of the British Royal Family who came to Japan have been to 'The Little House'.

Besides being Honorary Patron of the Japan-British Society, I was also Honorary Patron of the Japan-Sweden Society, and so in 1962 I paid a visit to both countries, as well as stopping over in Paris and Copenhagen.

It had been 25 years since the Prince and I had travelled so happily together by ship to attend King George VI's coronation in London, and now both men were no longer living, and here I was flying alone by air, bound for that nostalgic city. The intervening unfortunate war notwithstanding, nothing had changed in the warmth with which the Royal Family and friends and acquaintances welcomed me. I was greatly touched to have the Dame Grand Cross of the Order of the British Empire bestowed upon me, and felt a renewed sense of responsibility in my capacity as Honorary Patron of the Japan-British Society, and my duty to nurture good relations between our two countries.

On this trip I was able to do things of personal significance I had long dreamed of. I had been unable to accompany the Prince to Oxford the time before. I shall never forget the thrill of finally being able to see for myself the place that had meant so much to him in his young days. To see the same great elms in the grounds, beneath which deer still roamed, and the minnows swimming in the same little River Cherwell. His old Magdalen College rooms were exactly the same as he had described them to me in detail so many times. As I touched the desk and the chair, it seemed as if he had only just left there. What moved me most deeply was to discover that he had replicated the arrangement of the furniture exactly in his study in both our Tokyo residence and in Gotemba.

I met scouts who remembered the Prince, and I saw the library, and the hall where he had received his degree. I also went to University College and saw the cherry tree planted by the present Emperor when he visited it as Crown Prince. How happy he would be, I thought, when I told him on my return how tall it had grown. I lunched with Dr Bouse, the President of Magdalen College, where the guests included my brother Ichiro, who was working in a bank in London, and Kazuko Asō, daughter of Prime Minister Shigeru Yoshida.

Five years later, I visited England again for an eleven-day visit to take part in the 75th anniversary celebrations of the Japan Society. As I arrived at Heathrow on 27 January 1967, I could see lots of familiar faces there to welcome me including several friends of the Prince's from his Oxford days now active in politics, who later arranged for me to attend a parliamentary debate. I remember how they looked up and smiled, as I sat in the Visitor's Gallery.

Five hundred people – Japanese, British, and members of the Royal Family – came to the Anniversary Dinner at the Savoy Hotel. I said, 'To see me here, looking so happy, surrounded by all of you, must be making the Prince jealous!' My remark was greeted by warm, spontaneous laughter. I know everyone wished he could have been there with us.

I felt like the princess in the film *Roman Holiday* when friends took me to a pub – something I could never dream of doing in Japan – although the Prince had told me how people looked the other way if the Prince of Wales chose to buy sandwiches from late-night street stalls. The British, he said, feel that even royalty have a right to privacy.

It was a great thrill to find the riverside house in Walton-on-Thames where I was born and spent my first eight months. It had not changed at all. I just gazed at it from the outside for a long time. I spent my last day on the beautiful, picturesque Isle of Wight with old friends. Passing the night in their old fourteenth century stone house, I felt as if I were part of a romantic tale of long ago. We could see the white chalk cliffs of southern England as we took a walk next morning. As I left for the airport, I felt how strong the bonds were that bound me to Britain, and I hoped Peace would last forever and that I would be able to come back again.

In April 1969 I received the Order of the Seraphim from the King of Sweden, and in October, I was asked to became Honorary Patron of the Traffic Accident Orphans Scholarship Society. My days were already full with activities connected with the Anti-Tuberculosis Association, my two international friendship societies, and the various cultural and sports organizations I had inherited the honorary patronage of from the Prince, but we had no children, and I no longer had to look after the Prince, and felt he would want me to do something more in the way of welfare work to benefit society, so I accepted. Time sped by for me like the proverbial arrow, which helped me cope with the grief of losing my beloved mother.

In 1971, their Majesties the Shōwa Emperor and Empress made their world tour. It was a dream the Emperor had long entertained, ever since his European tour as Prince Regent in 1921. My fervent prayers for a safe journey for them were embodied in my farewell gift to Their Majesties of a tiny ornamental tiger, an animal traditionally said to travel 'A thousand leagues there and a thousand leagues back.' From everything I heard, the Emperor's simple, unaffected sincerity, and the Empress's warm smile earned them respect and affection wherever they went. It was marvellous being able to follow Their Majesties' journey daily on television. How the Prince would have enjoyed that! He had only seen TV transmissions in their experimental stage.

I was built a lovely, comfortable new house in 1972. Although of concrete, it is a Japanese-style bungalow, designed by the architect Isoya Yoshida. It is only about half as large as the house the Prince and I lived in before the fire-bombing, but seemed enormous to me after 'The Little House'. While it was being built, I feared the wild pheasants I use to feed would forget all about me, but to my delight, they were soon back. It took us humans a little longer to get used to the new house, with its air conditioning and other modern conveniences. 'If only the Prince were here!' my servants and I would say to one another. 'What would he make of it all?'

November saw the publication of 'The Life of Prince Yasuhito' based on his diaries and papers, which I had asked the Prince's old mountaineering friend and distinguished journalist Saburō Matsukata to compile and edit. It must have been no easy task to go through the vast amount of material and sift out the facts with meticulous care and produce such a readable and complete portrait of the Prince. It was something I had wanted as a memorial to him, and the completion of the book filled me with great emotion. It had taken Saburō Matsukata fifteen years, during which time he not only led a Mount Everest expedition, but was seriously ill.

## TEA WITH THE QUEEN MOTHER

In 1974, I was invited by the British Government to
visit England again. Sadly, news of the Duke of
Gloucester's grave illness coincided with my departure, and the invitation to spend one night with them
had to be cancelled. I had rather dreaded the news
conference at the Japanese Embassy on my first day,
fearing some awkward questions about Japan's reaction
to the oil crisis and the Labour government in Britain,
but the young journalists could not have been nicer.
After another nostalgic visit to Oxford, it was with a
heavy heart that I visited Kensington Palace to offer my
condolences on the death of the Duke of Gloucester.

That evening's dinner given for me by the Government went on as scheduled, and in the four days up to
the funeral, no royal engagements were cancelled,
from lunch with the Queen at Buckingham Palace to
tea with the Queen Mother. The kindness and
consideration of the Royal Family and the warmth of
their hospitality in spite of being in mourning, touched
me deeply, and was a revelation to me. Even Alice,
Duchess of Gloucester, the day before the Duke's
funeral, sent a message to say she would like to see me.
She looked so worn and emaciated after all she had
been through that I could not keep back my tears. Our
mutual loss seemed to bind us together more deeply
than ever. I attended the Duke's funeral next day in St.
George's Chapel at Windsor Castle.

I had tea with the Queen Mother at Clarence House
after lunching with the Queen. She was dressed in
black, and the lavender stock, arranged in a beautiful
vase, gave a suggestion of mourning. The camera and
Japanese vase I had brought her were already displayed
on a table. I explained that the vase was the work of

Yaichi Kusube, and that the camera produced the date on each photograph taken. It was then a novelty and Her Majesty seemed much intrigued.

No-one waited on us. The Queen Mother herself served me with tea, bread-and-butter, tomato sandwiches, and *petit fours*. We had not met since the late King George VI's Coronation 37 years before, so there was plenty to talk about. She was anxious to know whether the Emperor and Empress had really and truly enjoyed their visit to Britain the previous year. She seemed relieved when I assured her that they still spoke of it often, fondly recalling memories. She appeared to have a great affection and admiration for the Japanese Imperial Family. She gave me a little china powder box when I left. What touched me most deeply was the fact that there were no other guests, enabling us to enjoy a lovely, leisurely heart-to-heart conversation over tea. I admired the beautiful climbing roses in her garden, and was able to tell her of my visit the previous day to Hampton Court to see the hundred peonies given by our Emperor and Empress. They were doing so well I thought their colour and fragrance – unique among oriental flowers – might make them a star attraction there in years to come. I said I knew Their Majesties would be delighted to hear how the peonies were flourishing.

My full schedule of engagements included a visit to the House of Lords, where Prince Charles happened to be giving his maiden speech as Prince of Wales. Having known him since he was a child, I was impressed by his youthful dignity and boldness of argument, his spirited embracing of the cause of youth, without being in the least affected or awkward. What promise! I thought, and was moved to tears. He spoke so frankly of his ideas about sports and leisure.

After attending the funeral of the Duke of Gloucester, I spent two delightful days in Scotland as the guest
of Sir William Keswick, flying there from London in an
aircraft of the Queen's Flight. He and his family lived in
Dumfries in a handsome white chalk manor house set
in a vast green pasture where cows grazed serenely.
From the moment I arrived, not only my host, but
everyone in the village wanted to know about 'Tomo-
san'. How was he? What was he doing now? By 'Tomo-
san' they meant His Imperial Highness Prince Tomohito of Mikasa, my nephew, of whom I have always
been very fond, and who calls me his favourite aunt.
The Keswicks looked after Prince Tomohito while he
was studying in England. He spent his holidays with
them, and was made to feel like one of the family. He
had told me how it was because of them and the people
of this village that he had learned to love and appreciate
Britain. I was delighted to find how fond they all were
of him. The villagers put on a show of Scottish dancing
with bagpipes especially for me, and I was persuaded
to dance, too. It was an unforgettable evening, under a
sky full of stars.

On 9 October 1978, at the British Embassy in Tokyo,
I was invested with the insignia of an Honorary Dame
Grand Cross of the Order of St Michael and St George
by Princess Margaret acting on behalf of the Queen. It
was an undeserved honour, which I consider was really
bestowed on the late Prince Chichibu and the Japan-
British Society he had represented, rather than on me,
and symbolized the close ties between our two
countries that began half a century ago.

The following year, I was invited to London again.
After a busy ten days mostly filled with official
engagements but which included a delightful three-
day stay with the Duchess of Gloucester and her family

at their country seat, I flew home via Washington, D.C. and a nostalgic visit to my old school and classmates. I was met at the airport by my young nephew Prince Norihito – then of Mikasa, but now Takamado – who was studying in Canada. The old Embassy I lived in as a child had been replaced by a palatial new building, but the Friends School had not changed at all. All was just as I remembered, except that the Headmaster now was a man young enough to be my son. There was Mildred on the wisteria-enveloped veranda to welcome me with open arms. Although she had a beautiful daughter with her, the 51 years melted away and it seemed like yesterday that we sat with our desks side by side in the classroom. Many other old schoolmates were assembled there, too, for a wonderful, nostalgic party.

I was invited to England again in 1981 on the occasion of the opening of the Great Japan Exhibition at the Royal Academy, which coincided with the 90th anniversary of the Japan Society. Prince Charles and Crown Prince Akihito – the present Emperor – were the joint patrons, and I made a great many speeches. On my way home, I paid an especially nostalgic visit to Switzerland where, after officially calling on the International Red Cross and World Health Organisation in Geneva, I rode by funicular from Zermat to Gornergratt, to gaze at the Prince's beloved Matterhorn, of which I had heard so much. To see it with my own eyes was a dream come true.

Until now my travels had mostly been to Britain, and had never included Asia, but in 1985 I accepted an invitation from the Nepal Tuberculosis Prevention Association, and also visited Thailand.

'DO AS YOU PLEASE MORE'

Nowadays, I spend more time than ever in my rose garden. The Prince and I were both passionately fond of rose-growing, but had, of course, to abandon them for vegetables during the war. I learned from my British friends that in England you do not cut your roses and give them away, but invite friends to see them growing in your garden! I try to follow this custom, but do give bunches to those who are too old or infirm to come to me. Ever since the Prince died, I find growing roses keeps me from being lonely. Every morning, I gaze into their faces, and talk to my roses. They seem to appreciate your tender loving care, and will always produce fine blooms for you in return.

On account of my advanced age, I had asked to be excused from official duties, and when Crown Prince Akihito succeeded the late Shōwa Emperor in 1990, I put on my *robe décolletée* a few days before the 12 November Enthronement, and went to pay my respects to the new Emperor and Empress, but I did not attend the Enthronement ceremony or the receptions afterwards.

Although they were very busy, the Prince and Princess of Wales, who were among the representatives of 60 countries in Japan for the occasion, came to see me the day before the Enthronement. Prince Charles hugged me and greeted me with a kiss. 'Why aren't you coming to the ceremony?' he asked, urging, 'Do come! I'll look after you.' His reassuring words, so full of affection, not only encouraged me tremendously, but enabled me to know what it would be like to be gently rebuked by a son. Prince Charles always used to call me his 'Japanese grandmother'.

I decided then and there to attend one of the

morning tea-parties. They were divided into two sections – heads of state at the Emperor's Palace, and crown princes and other members of royalty at the Crown Prince's Palace. I attended the latter.

When I arrived, I found a table and chair had been provided just for me. How considerate of the young Crown Prince, I thought, and was immensely proud of the way he had grown into such a charming host. I had not expected so many people would come up and talk to me. I had a lovely time, and when Prince Charles appeared, his look of satisfaction as he watched me holding court made me suspect that he had had a hand in it, too.

The Prince and Princess of Wales were only in Japan four days, but I saw them three times. One of those times Prince Charles lectured me sternly.

'Your Highness, you should do as you please more, like our Queen Mother. You mustn't be so restrained, and so worried about what you do. Just do whatever you want. It'll be good for you.'

The Queen Mother was older than I, he told me, yet she was in fine health, and flew to France in her own aeroplane, or anywhere else she fancied. When I told him you cannot do that sort of thing in Japan – or rather I could not, he scolded me.

'Don't say you can't, just go ahead and do it!'

I smiled. But, silently, to herself, his 'Japanese grandmother' said, 'Thank you, Charles!'

The Prince of Wales had injured his right arm by a fall from his horse before coming to Japan. It was still painful, but he felt he should come, since there was no one to take his place. He kept his arm so cleverly concealed that no one noticed it during his stay in Japan. How I admired his sense of duty and responsibility!

My health has gradually improved and although I have passed my 80th birthday, I have begun to take up some of my public duties again. That same year that Akihito became Emperor, marking the end of the Shōwa reign and the beginning of the new reign called Heisei, the Japan Anti-Tuberculosis Association celebrated its fiftieth anniversary. I learned that over two hundred thousand people still suffered from the disease in this country, and eight million people each year were contracting it worldwide. How much there still was to be done! I remembered the words of Her Majesty, Empress Nagako – now the Empress Dowager – who had said to me, 'I know you will do your best.'

> *Mindful of her words,*
> *I am filled with new resolve.*
> *So much still to do.*
> *For in their various fields,*
> *So many have done so much.*

# *The Poems*

*Romanized version of the poems in the memoir*

Hachi no ume/sono ka mo kiyoku/nioedomo
Waga otōto no/Sugata wa miezu                 *p. 186/7*

Hahamiya mo/Kimi mo imasazu/Kyō yori wa
Nani o tanomite/Ikin kono yo o               *p. 187*

Kimi wa haya/Yo o sarimashinu/Hito mina ni
Kaku shitawaretsu/Oshimaretsu shite          *p. 187*

Tomosureba/Kuzuren to suru/Waga kokoro
Sasauru mono wa/Haha no minasake             *p. 187/8*

Tsune hi goro/Au ni aranedo/Haha imasu
Sono koto nomi ga/Tayori narishi o           *p. 188*

Kono yoi wo/Waga se no Miya wa/Hahamiya to
Izuku no sono ni/Katarimasuran               *p. 188*

Fuji mitemo/Kimi o zo omou/Mado chikaku
Kotori kiku ni mo/Kimi o zo omou             *p. 188*

Omoide wa/Koyonaku tanoshi/Yama ni umi ni
Totsu kuni ni sae/Tsuredachi shi hi no       *p. 188/9*

Mina ni hajizu/Ikin to zo omou/Itsu no hi ka
Kimi ga mimoto ni/Mesaruru hi made           *p. 189*

Nakebatote/Kaeranu kimi to/Shiri nagara
Hitoke naki yo wa/Namida ni kururu           *p. 189*

Mikotoba ni/Kokoro o shimete/Tsukushi koshi
Michi sorezore no/Hagemi o tatau             *p. 202*

# *Index*